Voluntary Accreditation:

A History of the North Central Association

1945-1970

by

LOUIS G. GEIGER

PROFESSOR OF HISTORY
THE COLORADO COLLEGE

THE NORTH CENTRAL ASSOCIATION
OF COLLEGES AND SECONDARY SCHOOLS

Publication Office:
George Banta Company, Menasha, Wisconsin 54952

Library of Congress Catalog Card Number: 76-118856

© *Copyright 1970 by the North Central Association of Colleges and Secondary Schools, Chicago, Illinois*

Printed in the United States of America

Contents

Foreword: The Association 1895–1945

To mark the 75th anniversary of the North Central Association of Colleges and Secondary Schools, we are presenting this history of the Association's activities for the past twenty-five years. Our historian, Louis G. Geiger, has spent almost three years in researching and writing this impressive book which should prove of value to our member institutions, to educators outside the North Central area, to present and future research scholars, and to those persons who are interested in what accreditation has meant for American education.

For those of you who have not read the earlier history of the Association,[1] may we briefly comment on the origins and development of this voluntary accrediting agency.

On March 29 and 30, 1895 thirty-six educators assembled at Northwestern University, Evanston, Illinois. They had come in response to an invitation to consider whether they wished "to organize, if deemed expedient, an association of colleges and secondary schools of the North Central States, representative of universities, colleges, scientific schools, normal schools, high schools, and academies."

The invitation was signed by these persons:

JAMES B. ANGELL, President, University of Michigan
HENRY WADE ROGERS, President, Northwestern University
CHARLES K. ADAMS, President, University of Wisconsin
WILLIAM R. HARPER, President, University of Chicago

1. Calvin O. Davis, *A History of the North Central Association*, Ann Arbor, Michigan, 1945 (hereafter cited as Davis).

W. H. Butts, Principal, Michigan Military Academy
W. A. Greeson, Principal, Grand Rapids High School
R. G. Boone, Principal, Michigan Normal School

The chief protagonist was William Butts of the Michigan Military Academy. Butts, a native of the East, had gone back for a visit in 1894 and learned while there about the newly organized New England Association of Colleges and Secondary Schools. On his return to Michigan, he favorably impressed several eminent educators with the idea of improving communication and relations through a formal association of high schools and institutions of higher education. At his behest, the Michigan Schoolmasters' Club became the sponsor of the organizational meeting.

Of the thirty-six individuals who attended the meeting, five were from Ohio, five from Michigan, four from Indiana, fourteen from Illinois, three from Wisconsin, three from Iowa, and two from Missouri. (No representatives were present from Minnesota, Nebraska, and Kansas although invitations had been sent to educators in those states.) Fourteen were presidents of universities, six were presidents of colleges, two were presidents of normal schools, one was a university professor, seven were representatives of the public school systems—two superintendents and five principals—and six were affiliated with private or church-related academies.

Informal discussions at the meeting focused on the purposes of the proposed association, drafting of a constitution, election of officers, and setting the date for the next meeting.

The first constitution stated that the "object of this Association shall be to establish closer relations between the colleges and the secondary schools of the North Central States." This objective has been a principal goal of the Association for the past seventy-five years.

During the early years of the Association, annual meetings took on the characteristics of scholarly seminars. The Executive Committee would suggest for discussion three or four controversial topics in the form of resolutions and would arrange for thoughtful presentations, brief prepared critiques, and general discussion on each issue. After heated and spirited debate, the resolution was adopted, modified, rejected, or referred to a special committee.

The following resolutions are still common concerns:

> RESOLVED, That in colleges, and especially in the larger universities, the tendency to intrust the freshman class to inexperienced teachers, often inferior to those in the high schools, is a growing evil and ought to be checked. (*Proceedings,* 1897, p. 10)

> RESOLVED, that the efficiency of the public schools in cities of considerable size is almost wholly contingent upon the framework of the organization under which they are managed and the legal status and functions of the officials charged with their care; that the system of government in such cities should be one that permits boards to exercise none but legislative functions and devolves executive duties and the appointment of subordinate officers and of teachers upon executive officers (*Proceedings,* 1899, p. ix).

Since Article IV of the Association's first constitution stated that "all decisions of the Association bearing upon the policy and the management of higher and of secondary institutions are understood to be advisory in their character," none of the resolutions had to be implemented. However, the intellectual stature of the participants in these annual discussions so impressed the delegates that they enthusiastically reported the deliberations and recommendations of the Association to their institutions and constituents.

Of major concern to the colleges and universities was the preparation of high school students for higher education. The University of Michigan had since 1871 employed a high school accrediting procedure by which professors would inspect Michigan schools and if the findings seemed satisfactory, these inspectors would recommend that the schools be accredited and that their graduates be admitted to the university without formal examination. Other states had adopted similar plans, but by 1900 it was recognized that students were crossing state lines in their choice of colleges, that high school standards and course offerings differed from state to state, and that there was need for common standards and curriculum.

In 1901 Dean F. A. Forbes of the University of Illinois presented the problem to the Association and urged the development of standards that would be acceptable to all institutions of higher education. The Association immediately appointed its first commission—The Commission on Accredited Schools. Three subcommittees were organized: 1) Committee on Unit Courses of Study; 2) Committee on High School Inspection; and 3) Committee on College Credit for High School Work.

The *Proceedings* of the Association are replete with reports from these committees. The recommended unit courses provided more than curriculum guides; they included detailed procedures, content, textbooks, and materials. The inspection committee developed criteria[2] which few high schools could meet and frankly announced that the accredited list would include very "select schools." The third committee struggled with a problem that still confronts us—advance placement and college credit for high school work.

When, at the 1903 annual meeting, the Commission recommended for accreditation an "honor list" of high schools, there was strong opposition from the floor. A. S. Draper, President of the University of Illinois, objected to the procedure on several bases including the attempt to standardize institutions; the notion of a select list which was "incomplete, biased, and indefensible"; and unfair pressure put on all schools in the area.[3] The list was returned to the Commission for further study. During the ensuing year, the Board of Inspectors sent a circular letter to all Association colleges and universities informing them of the aims and methods of the Board and seeking their full cooperation. A year later, a list of 156 schools was recommended for accreditation and these high schools were promptly approved by the Association.[4]

Curriculum development had been a major concern of the Association since 1898 when the Committee on the Teaching of

2. See Appendix, p. 186 for first published criteria.
3. Davis, p. 54.
4. See Appendix, pp. 185-186 for first list of accredited secondary schools.

English had been appointed. In 1903 the Committee on Unit Courses of Study presented outlines for various courses and in 1906 standing committees—of about twenty members each—were appointed to make annual revisions of unit courses in high school subjects.

These curriculum committees were undoubtedly influenced by several national agencies that were also attempting to answer the query, "What constitutes a high school and what constitutes a college?" (This question was the topic for discussion at NCA's first annual meeting.) President Henry King of Oberlin College, NCA's delegate to the Carnegie Foundation for the Advancement of Teaching, reported to the 1907 annual meeting that the Foundation was planning to give retirement funds under certain conditions to professors in an accepted list of colleges and universities. In determining the accepted institutions, the Foundation had issued an arbitrary definition of what constitutes a college.

Among the necessary items was the requirement for admission of not less than four years of high school preparation designated in terms of units, a unit being a course of five periods weekly throughout an academic year. Fourteen such units would constitute minimum preparation for college entrance. King stated that the definitions of units were in close accordance with the requirements of the College Entrance Examination Board.[5]

In 1908 the report of the NCA Committee on Unit Courses replicated the Carnegie Foundation definition with one exception: the minimum graduate requirement of the high school and the entrance requirement of the college became fifteen units. (The "Carnegie Unit," thus established, for years has been the basic measure for course offerings; only recently have secondary schools felt free to break this so-called "lock-step.") At the same meeting, the Committee expanded programs of study to include not only the "academic subjects" such as English, mathematics, history, classical and romance languages, and the physical sciences, but also the commercial subjects, mechanical arts, and

5. *NCA Proceedings*, 1907, pp. 61-65.

household arts. This action connotes the Association's first recorded concern for students who were unlikely to attend college and for the schools that were striving to give these students marketable skills. It was the Association's first acknowledgement that diversity was possible in quality schools that attempted to educate students with varying interests and abilities.

For several years, the Board of Inspectors was solely concerned with standardizing and inspecting high schools but when the beneficial effects of the Board's activities became evident, members of the Association raised the question, "Why not also standardized colleges and universities?"[6] Proponents of this point of view gradually grew in number, and in March 1906 the accrediting commission's name was changed to Commission on Accredited Schools and Colleges and it was instructed to report on the advisability of initiating a plan for the inspection and accreditation of colleges and universities. A set of standards was first presented at the annual meeting in 1908 when the membership suggested a number of revisions. In 1909 the Commission returned with several changes in the criteria which were then approved.[7] (Again the relationship between the NCA, the Carnegie Foundation, and the College Entrance Examination Board could be noted in these standards.)

The Commission promptly appointed a committee of five to supervise and direct this new undertaking, each state was asked to establish a college inspection board, and the process for accrediting colleges was established. In 1913 the first list of accredited colleges was published.[8]

The North Central Association was no longer just a debating society providing an annual forum for discussion of current issues. As Davis reports:

> From this period forth, the North Central Association was a power in education, exerting its influence directly upon schools and colleges within its own territory, but indirectly

6. Davis, p. 57.
7. See Appendix, p. 188.
8. See Appendix, p. 187.

affecting educational thought and practice throughout the country. It now began adopting administrative policies and setting academic standards that were enforceable. To be sure, its regulations still nominally affected no institution outside its own membership circle, but Association membership now became such a prized honor that few schools or colleges eligible to recognition were willing, in any way, to endanger their chances of being so affiliated. Hence, all of them listened with deep concern whenever the Association spoke. Indeed, to be omitted from that organization's roster was soon regarded as one of the more serious misfortunes that could befall such an institution.[9]

The accrediting criteria for high schools were frequently revised as inspectors reported on the variety of factors that affected the quality of a school. Soon the standards covered almost every facet of educational administration, facilities, and program.

In 1916 a separate commission was created to consider matters relating to higher institutions. The new Commission on Institutions of Higher Education devoted several years to the study of special problems in accreditation and made some broad changes in 1918 when institutions of higher learning were grouped into three different divisions—colleges and universities, junior colleges, and teacher training institutions—and a distinct set of criteria was established for each division.

During the ensuing years, accrediting standards for all types of institutions were frequently revised and refined as circumstances seemed to warrant. However, despite the numerous changes and additions, the standards seemed inadequate for measuring the effectiveness of educational institutions. Criticisms were voiced about certain published standards and methods of enforcement; formal, arbitrary, and *ex parte* criteria for judging an institution's quality; failure to strike a balance between the weaknesses and strengths in an institution's program; no recognition of unique or special aims of an institution; and overemphasis on quantitative rather than qualitative factors.[10]

9. Davis, pp. 45-46.
10. *Ibid.*, pp. 69-70.

In 1929 the Higher Commission initiated a study which would revolutionize accrediting policies and practices. The Commission appointed a Committee on Revision of Standards comprised of fifteen knowledgeable college administrators[11] and charged them with the responsibility of (1) evaluating the NCA standards and accrediting procedures and (2) developing new criteria for the measurement of institutions.

With the assistance of five experts[12] the committee developed a project plan, secured funds with which to finance the study ($110,000 from the Rockefeller General Education Board, $25,000 from the Association, and about $5,000 from a special assessment of $25 from each NCA college and university), and enlisted the cooperation of a representative group of fifty-seven higher institutions in the NCA area.[13] These institutions supplied comprehensive information through questionnaires and conducted an extensive testing program under the direction of the committee. The several representatives of the committee subsequently visited each of the institutions to obtain additional information and impressions which provided the basic findings for the report. The committee chairman, President L. D. Coffman, University of Minnesota, stated in his report to the Commission that "the committee engaged in a very careful and extensive program of research in which modern statistical methods played an important part. The detailed manner in which this attempt was carried on, the constructive proposals that have been made, and the forms or patterns devised for estimating the worth of higher institutions are all set forth clearly and fully in the volumes of this report."[14]

The newly developed philosophy which undergirds regional

11. Davis, footnote, p. 70.
12. *Ibid.*, p. 70.
13. George F. Zook and M. E. Haggerty, *The Evaluation of Higher Institutions: Principles of Accrediting Higher Institutions.* Preface by L. D. Coffman, p. vi.
14. The full report was published by the University of Chicago Press. The seven volumes included: *Principles of Accrediting Higher Institutions* by Zook and Haggerty (1936); *The Faculty* by Melvin E. Haggerty (1937); *The Educational Program* by Haggerty (1937); *The Library* by Douglas Waples (1936);

and professional accrediting to this day was embodied in the committee's report which stated that "an institution will be judged for accreditment upon the basis of the total pattern it presents as an institution of higher education . . . it is recognized that wide variations will appear . . . the facilities and activities of an institution will be judged in terms of the purposes it seeks to serve."[15]

Concurrently the Commission on Secondary Schools was planning a similar study related to its accrediting problems. Criticisms of published high school standards had been numerous and insistent for more than a decade when in 1933 the NCA Secondary Commission proposed a nationwide investigation of secondary school accrediting under the direction of all the regional accrediting associations.

Plans were formulated for an extensive cooperative study of secondary school standards and accrediting procedures supervised by a General Committee of twenty-one members selected from the six regional agencies, which had been established by that time, and advisory members representing the American Council on Education, the National Committee on Research in Secondary Education, the National Education Association, the NCA Committee on Revision of Standards for Higher Education, and the United States Office of Education. Again, the Rockefeller General Education Board made a generous grant to help fund the project and each of the regional associations allocated funds in proportion to its financial resources. The study extended over a period of five years and cost approximately $200,000.

The purposes of the study were expressed or implied in the following questions:

1. What are the characteristics of a good school?
2. What practical means and methods may be employed to

Student Personnel Service by Donfred H. Gardner (1936); *Administration* by John Dale Russell and Floyd W. Reeves (1936); and *Finance* by Russell and Reeves (1937).

15. Zook and Haggerty, *Principles of Accrediting Higher Institutions,* p. 98.

evaluate the effectiveness of a school in terms of its objectives?

3. By what means and processes does a good school develop into a better one?

4. How can regional associations stimulate secondary schools to continuous growth?[16]

Procedures for the study included the development of an extensive set of tentative evaluative criteria, a self-testing program for each school, an intensive survey of two hundred selected schools, ongoing revision of the evaluative criteria after reviewing trial results, and the adoption of a revised plan of accrediting. Like the Higher Commission, the NCA Commission on Secondary Schools and its counterparts in the other regions sought to measure the effectiveness of a school by placing more emphasis on the "total pattern" of the institution rather than relying on sets of isolated formal standards. Quantitative standards continued to be published and used but they no longer constituted the sole basis for judging the quality of a school.

In 1940 the Cooperative Study of Secondary School Standards published the first edition of *Evaluative Criteria*. Its opening paragraph entitled "Statement of Guiding Principles" immediately followed by "Suggestions for Formulation and Statements of Philosophy and Objectives" stressed the importance of adopting goals which would meet "the needs of the pupil population and community which the school serves." Standardization had given way and diversity was recognized in its stead.

The Cooperative Study of Secondary School Standards (now called the National Study of School Evaluation) has been a continuous force for the improvement of secondary education and revised editions of *Evaluative Criteria* have been published each decade—1950, 1960, and 1970. The instrument has been widely used for self-evaluation of schools and is still used for review by NCA visiting teams.[17]

16. E. D. Grizell, "The Cooperative Study of Secondary School Standards," *North Central Association Quarterly* XII (July 1937) pp. 34-44.

17. John A. Stanavage, "NCA Administrators' Reactions to School Evaluation," Table I, "Schools Evaluated, Instruments Used, Rating of Instruments," *NCAQ,* XLIV (Fall, 1969) p. 231.

When the Association adopted a revised constitution in 1916, the Committee on Unit Courses of Study became a separate Commission on Unit Courses and Curricula. The new Commission's assignment was to "define unit courses of study in various subjects and to consider the curriculum and organization of all classes of institutions included within the Association."

The Committee's earlier activities had been concerned almost solely with instructional materials; however, the new Commission turned its attention to administrative problems which affected the quality of the curriculum. In 1918 subcommittees were formed to survey the following areas:

1. The organization of faculty and pupils for cooperative action.
2. The social organization of the school body.
3. The curriculum organization—traditional or functional?
4. The supervision of teachers.
5. Educational and vocational guidance.
6. The use of statistics as bases for administrative policies.
7. Library administration.
8. Athletic policies.

At the same time, the Commission sought to develop qualitative standards for the evaluation of units of instruction, and in 1924 the Commission issued a 48-page report of its efforts (Part III of 1924 *Proceedings*). Continuing its curriculum-making leadership, the Commission prepared and published in 1933 a 400-page book on *High School Curriculum Reorganization* which embodied all the analyses and recommendations of the Commission. Two thousand copies of this book were printed and sold in a few months after publication.

Like the two accrediting commissions, the Commission on Unit Courses and Curriculum directed its efforts toward securing diversity in curriculum policies—diversity determined primarily by the needs of individual pupils and local community interests. The Commission established a Committee on Experimental Units to encourage school experimentation involving such matters as: fusing, integrating, or correlating courses, e.g., English and social studies, mathematics and science, art and music, physical education and practical arts; establishing core curriculums; modifying the length of class periods; varying the methods of instruction; and organizing entirely new teaching materials. Ultimately a whole new series of experimental units was developed by the Commission, tested and retested in the schools, and published and distributed.

The Commission also initiated a Committee on Curriculum Trends to collect information about innovations in member secondary schools; a Committee on Functional Organization of the Secondary Schools to encourage schools to establish their programs upon a realistic basis rather than an "academic" basis; a Committee on General Education to make certain that all high school students received a background of general education in addition to vocational or college preparatory courses;[18] and a Committee on the Preparation of Secondary School Teachers to study the training—academic and professional—of high school teachers. In 1942, this committee became affiliated with a nationwide study sponsored by the American Council on Education and financed by the Rockefeller General Education Board.

This study emphasized and made apparent the need for supplementary review of the many factors involved in preparation programs for high school teachers. The Commission established several committees to work with teacher-preparation institutions, with student teaching programs, with teacher certification agencies, and with high schools that were conducting in-service education of teachers. From these studies came the Liberal Arts Study and the Teacher Education Project which are still making valuable contributions to teacher preparation.

When the NCA Constitution was amended in 1942, the Commission on Unit Courses and Curriculum became the Commission on Research and Service. Under Article IV, Section 6, the Commission was charged with the responsibility of initiating, planning, and carrying forward "studies in the field of educational and institutional research and service pertaining to uni-

18. After three or four years of study, this committee published a book entitled *General Education in the American High School*. (Chicago: Scott, Foresman and Company, 1942).

versities, colleges, and secondary schools" conceived by the Commission, the Executive Committee, or either of the other commissions.

With this background of the first fifty years (1895-1945) of the Association's endeavors, we present Louis G. Geiger's narrative account of the Association's past twenty-five years. To this effort Geiger has brought the analytic insights of a historian who, though never previously affiliated with the NCA, has objectively scanned the Association's records to provide a most readable account of the latter third of its life span. The NCA Board of Directors and its Committee on Publications and Information Service have given him a free hand in his writing, except for leads on available contacts, on sequence of events, and on possible emphases.

Geiger has not only recorded NCA's attempts, successes, and frustrations (we hesitate to call them failures), but he has related these programs to the social climate of the time. We are indeed grateful to him for undertaking this task and for producing this history of the activities of the North Central Association of Colleges and Secondary Schools (1945-1970).

ROBERT J. KELLER, Chairman
NCA Committee on Publications
and Information Service

University of Minnesota
Minneapolis, Minnesota
March, 1970

Preface and Acknowledgements

Social historians long ago pointed out that one of the most distinguishing characteristics of the American social order is the large role played by voluntary, nonofficial, nongovernmental organizations. It is not too much to say that this "association-ism," or "joinerism," is in many respects the cement of American life, and a major activating force as well. Some historians of the communist world[1] have even observed that the prominence of self-generative activity in the western countries is the major difference between them and eastern or "third world" states, and that its absence almost requires a resort to statism and dictatorship.

In the United States this principle of voluntary association has not only provided local services and amenities, but it has also exerted powerful influences in the management of major functions in the society, one of them being the education of its citizens. As everyone knows, the American education "system" is not a system at all in the sense of centralized organization, but rather fifty systems, one for each state. Moreover, these are further divided by the variations of the individual districts, the extensive parochial establishments, and a considerable number of private institutions of one sort or another. Yet, it is also true that American education is very much the same from one end of the continent to another.

1. See, for example, Theodore H. Von Laue, *Why Lenin? Why Stalin?* (Philadelphia: J. B. Lippincott and Co., 1964); *The Global City* (Lippincott, 1969).

In part, of course, this uniformity is simply a reflection of the uniformity of national goals and aspirations, and of American life itself. The structures of state governments, for example, are remarkably similar although there is nothing which specifically requires them to be so. Emulation and custom also exert no small influence upon educational practice, but the most direct force for uniformity has come from the voluntary accrediting associations composed of representatives of the educational establishment itself. Associations have taken a variety of forms, such as the associations of the more prestigious universities, the land-grant colleges, the junior colleges, the associations of individual academic disciplines (the American Chemical Society, for example), and the six general regional accrediting associations. The latter, which include all levels of institutions except the elementary schools,[2] have assumed, or have had abandoned to them, the responsibility of evaluating educational performance in the United States. In effect, these voluntary, self-generating bodies of educators shape the nation's schools. The result is a peculiar blend of autonomy and uniformity, and something uniquely American.

Of these regional accrediting bodies, none has been more active and more influential than the North Central Association of Colleges and Secondary Schools. It covers a larger and more varied geographical area and probably enjoys a larger measure of public confidence and general prestige than any other association. In many respects, therefore, a history of the NCA is a history of voluntary accreditation, with some allowances for variations of emphasis and influence from one region to another.

My own interest in the regional associations is that of the social historian who has come to educational history by the social history route, rather than from the discipline of Education. When the NCA Publications Committee invited me to study the records of the NCA and to write its history, the opportunity was as important to a historian with my interests as the chance to explore

2. Recently, the Southern Association of Colleges and Schools initiated the accreditation of elementary schools.

for the first time the papers of a major political personage or governmental or business institution would be for others.

The Board of Directors and the three commissions, and especially their executive secretaries, gave me full access to their records and encouraged me to attend meetings of the commissions and the various committees to enable me to form my own impressions of the people who manage the Association, their methods, their concerns, and their capabilities. I have talked at length with Norman Burns, executive secretary of the Association and of the Commission on Colleges and Universities, to Mrs. Anne Stameshkin, associate secretary of the Association, and to Gordon Cawelti, Secretary of the Commission on Secondary Schools until May 1969. All of them have read the manuscript entirely or in part. Their collective memories and long experience as educators and as officials of the Association have been invaluable. Mrs. Stameshkin also contributed editorial advice and undertook that onerous chore, the index. The office personnel in the Association headquarters cheerfully hauled out dusty records, photocopied documents, provided supplies, saw to my comfort, and in other ways made my several extended stays in the NCA offices as pleasant as they were useful. I am also much in the debt of the librarians of Colorado College, especially Miss Rita Ridings, Reference Librarian at the Tutt Library.

Others with a long and devoted experience in the affairs of the Association who have read all or part of the manuscript include Richard W. Burkhardt, Vice President and Dean of Faculties, Ball State University (Commission on Research and Service); Frank S. Endicott, Professor of Education and Director of Placement, Northwestern University (Commission on Research and Service); Lowell B. Fisher, Coordinator, University-School Articulation, University of Illinois (Commission on Secondary Schools); Alva J. Gibson, Executive Secretary, Commission on Secondary Schools (1953-1962); Edgar Johnston, Bureau of School Services, University of Michigan (Commission on Secondary Schools); Robert J. Keller, Dean, College of Education, University of Minnesota (Chairman of the NCA Committee on

Publications; Commission on Secondary Schools; and Commission on Colleges and Universities); Walter C. Langsam, President, University of Cincinnati (Commission on Colleges and Universities); Robert J. Mulligan, S.J., Vice President and Dean of Faculties, Loyola University (Commission on Colleges and Universities); Stephen A. Romine, Dean, College of Education, University of Colorado (Commission on Secondary Schools and Commission on Colleges and Universities); John A. Stanavage, Executive Secretary (since June 1969), Commission on Secondary Schools; and W. Fred Totten, Director of Graduate Study, Mott Program of the Flint, Michigan Board of Education (Commission on Research and Service).

As usual, my wife, Helen, has given much assistance in research and reading manuscript. Perhaps more important for the development of this history, she has listened to innumerable trial runs of ideas about the regulation of American education through voluntary associations. Finally I owe a special debt of gratitude to George W. Starcher, President of the University of North Dakota (consultant-examiner for the Commission on Colleges and Universities) who was the matchmaker between me and the North Central Association.

LOUIS G. GEIGER
Colorado Springs, Colorado
December 15, 1969

Fiftieth Anniversary:
A War Ends and a New Era Begins

World War II had not quite ended when the North Central
Association of Colleges and Secondary Schools reached its fiftieth
anniversary in 1945. Because of war-time restrictions on travel,
the annual general meeting of the Association was again postponed, and official celebration of the Association's golden anniversary was limited to the publication of its first history, which had
been prepared by Calvin O. Davis, editor of the *Quarterly*.[1]

The Association could look back with no little satisfaction
upon its fifty years of existence. It had won the respect of the
high schools, the colleges and universities, and the general public
in a huge twenty-state[2] area extending across mid-America from
West Virginia to Arizona. It was the largest of the six regional
accrediting associations and was generally acknowledged to be
the most prestigious and the most innovative as well. "Accredited
by the North Central Association" had become the essential recognition for high schools and colleges. Three hundred ten colleges in the NCA area had won approval by 1945, and those
which had not achieved accreditation coveted and strove mightily
for it. Of the high schools in the region, 3,033 were accredited.
Since a smaller percentage of high schools than colleges was ap-

---

1. Calvin O. Davis, *A History of the North Central Association of Colleges
and Secondary Schools, 1895-1945* (Ann Arbor, 1945).
2. The Montana schools, which first appeared on the 1910 list of accredited
institutions, withdrew in 1951 to join the Northwest Association.

1

proved, the company of the accredited was even more exclusive in secondary circles. And although they might not know what accreditation stood for exactly, school boards and parents in a public school district were likely to attach more importance to approval than the principals and teachers who were directly concerned.

Equally encouraging to the governing bodies of the NCA and to those who had labored for years to bring it to a role of prestige and power was the fact that the NCA and the educational establishment it represented were emerging from a decade and a half of crisis. First, there was the great depression when crippling financial stringencies had inevitably set back educational standards, or at least slowed advancement. Then followed World War II when military demands had decimated the ranks of qualified teachers on every educational level, had transformed colleges and universities into virtual female establishments, and even more than the depression had cut off financial resources for buildings, equipment, and salaries. Hopefully, a time for recovery and settling down had arrived. It was not to be so, however, for in 1945, American education entered an era of continuing change unmatched since the battle for free public schools had been fought and won a century before.

The prolonged crisis was not the shattering experience it might have been for the schools largely because of the regional accrediting associations. The North Central Association had steadily expanded its activites and influence during the depression. And when World War II began, it was better prepared for that emergency than for the two previous wars the Association had weathered. The Spanish-American War, short as it was and coming soon after the organization of the Association, appears to have had almost no effect nor to have elicited any response. World War I, a much larger conflict, found the NCA scarcely better prepared to adjust to the emergency and to provide the proper leadership to its constituent colleges and secondary schools. If the NCA or any other of the regional associations came forward with an imaginative veterans' adjustment proposal, it has not been recorded. A few brave resolutions seem to have been about the best the NCA could manage.[3]

It was much different in World War II. The "great debate" over the American role in the European war had alerted educational leaders to the possibility of mobilization; moreover, by the 1940's the Association was firmly established and alive to the prospective problems for education generally and to the responsibilities of schools and colleges in an emergency. No one doubted that this war would bring a more nearly total mobilization of natural and human resources than Americans had ever experienced. Nor did anyone doubt that the educational establishment would have a central role in mobilizing manpower and brains. The public and especially the national government and its military establishment were agreed in the expectation that the schools would be enlisted in the great war effort when it came.

Formal involvement in the war, from December 1941 to August 1945, was longer by far than either the brief summer excursion of 1898 or World War I, and had a proportionately greater effect on the high schools and colleges of the United States. The North Central Association acknowledged its responsibility and attempted to meet it without delay. Although no specific measures seem to have been prepared in anticipation of the formal war declaration, the issue of national defense had at least been the subject of preliminary discussions. At the annual meeting in March 1940, and again the following year, Irving Maurer, president of the Association, warned the members of the challenge of German and Japanese imperialism,[4] and the contemporary issues of the *Quarterly* also contain numerous references to the schools' responsibilities in the event of war.

When war finally came the Association immediately curtailed its own "non-essential" activities. In October 1942 the Commission on Secondary Schools set a two-day limit on its business at the annual meeting and agreed also that no efforts would be

3. Davis, pp. 142-143.
4. Editorial, *North Central Association Quarterly (NCAQ)*, XIX (October 1944), pp. 146-147.

made to secure attendance of any other than Commission members. The 1945 annual meeting of the Association was cancelled entirely, even though it was the Golden Anniversary year.

Less than a month after Pearl Harbor, the Executive Committee of the Association, following a hurried meeting in Chicago (January 10, 1942), issued a circular to all member schools and colleges reminding them that they would best serve the nation by continuing as near a normal program as possible and by encouraging young people to stay in school unless they were needed elsewhere by their country. The NCA offered encouragement and assistance to institutions which found it necessary to accelerate programs, but it urged that such speedups not be undertaken at the price of "diluting" good quality. In early 1943 the Association's Executive Committee ruled that no new colleges would be accredited for the duration of the conflict, and review boards were advised to exercise great care in suspending member institutions. Despite the frequent admonitions that standards must not be lowered, the automatic extension of all memberships in 1945, when the annual meeting's cancellation was announced, said plainly enough that winning the war came ahead of accreditation.

Probably the most serious problem for the schools during this time was the ever-growing teacher shortage. This had already become a matter of concern as early as 1940 when the Committee of Seven (then the name of the executive body) of the Commission on Secondary Schools voted that vacancies occasioned by the war could be filled by unqualified persons as an emergency measure but only for the duration of the war. Schools were put on "warning" if they were employing unqualified teachers, but in 1943 even this was modified to the milder "advisement." Meantime, an official circular from the Association, approved in March 1942, urged state-wide surveys of teacher supply, the recruitment of educated people not originally trained for teaching, recruitment of married women (who had almost disappeared from the public schools during the depression because of spread-the-work practices and the view that a married woman could not devote full time to teaching), supplemental training of active teachers to fit them to teach subjects in which the worst shortages occurred, and finally a general relaxation of special state regulations in order to enable teachers to migrate freely. The Association also requested that Federal manpower agencies consider teachers as essential personnel and hence exempt from military duty.

An issue of almost equal immediacy was the granting of credit for military experience. Although high school and college students faced by the draft were hopeful of some transferable academic credit for their military service, educators generally were wary of repeating the emotionally inspired and generally unsatisfactory policies which followed World War I, when large amounts of academic credit had been awarded on a time-in-service basis. It was agreed, however, that military training, especially training in service schools, should be evaluated on an equivalency to credit basis. The NCA took the lead among regional associations in developing a realistic policy. On January 12, 1942, the Executive Committee endorsed the granting of college credit not to exceed one-half a semester's credit for the completion of basic training and suggested that such credits be counted as physical education, hygiene, or electives. It also urged accelerating students' educational standing on the basis of demonstrated ability and recommended examinations to determine the level of achievement.

The Commission on Secondary Schools simultaneously recommended that veterans attending high school receive varying amounts of credit for portions of semesters interrupted by military duty; a year of service was to be counted as equivalent to two units of credit; up to two units were to be allowed also for validated special training in a trade, in foreign languages, in mathematics, and in the physical sciences.[5] In November 1942 the Association announced a general policy of recognizing credit for competence demonstrated through performance on specially prepared examinations.[6] These policies were formalized with a

5. A. J. Brumbaugh, "Accreditation of Military Experience," *NCAQ*, XXI (January 1947), p. 298.
6. Davis, p. 144.

few variations by the American Council on Education when it undertook the establishment of uniform practices for the nation. The NCA also took the lead in working out a systematic evaluation policy for instruction taken in the proliferating service education program, especially in the United States Armed Forces Institute (USAFI). A 1500-page *Guide* on the subject was developed for schools and colleges.

What such policies meant in practice was that academic credit was given chiefly for training that might fit into a high school or college program. From this start, and in line with an American Council on Education study, there evolved a general national policy and formalized practice in recognition of the USAFI. Many NCA colleges, despite some murmurs of disapproval from the Association, carried the matter further by accepting some veterans entirely on the basis of examination. Although there was no official Association sanction for this practice, the Secondary Commission accepted it in 1946 with the provision that a standardized test be used and that a minimum score be achieved.

In many respects the pressures of the war did much to soften rigidities in accreditation practices and requirements. Educational acceleration or the measurement of achievement by tests instead of by units or diploma; new teaching methods and objectives, exemplified particularly in the languages; and the introduction of new subjects—the Asiatic languages for example—proved to be not only feasible but necessary and long overdue.[7]

On the other hand, there were such questionable tendencies as the armed services' effort to direct education toward short-term demands of the war at the expense of humane and social objectives. Although Congress showed little inclination to dictate educational practices, being content to leave this jurisdiction to state and local agencies, various administrative departments and the armed services were less forebearing. The Navy, for example, urged increased attention to health, mathematics, and physics. The Air Force wanted special emphasis given to elementary aero-

7. "What Schools and Colleges Can Learn from Education in the Armed Forces," *NCAQ*, XXI (October 1946), pp. 220-234.

nautics, military customs and traditions, the use of tools, and mathematics and physics. The Army wanted the schools to provide training in radio operation, auto mechanics, and other vocational fields. In fact, lesson plans and various materials for teaching such courses were prepared for the schools. Most ominous of all was the pressure to emphasize the production of "confident, alert, loyal, brave, and healthy men who will be able to give orders and to obey them."[8]

Indicative of the atmosphere prevailing were the titles of two major addresses at the annual NCA meetings in 1943 and 1944: "What the Army Wants in Pre-Induction Training," and "The Effects of the War Effort on the High School." The numerous pamphlets distributed to the schools by the armed services included such titles as "Is Your Number Up?" "Attention! To Your Health," "Training Through Recreation," and "Higher Education and the National Defense."[9]

Whatever dangers there may have been in such tendencies were counteracted, however, by the decentralization of the American school system, the generally liberal spirit that pervaded it, the natural inertia of any institution, and by the fact that the war came to an end within a reasonable time. In fact, the positive gains of considerable experimentation with teaching method and curricular innovation, often long overdue, may have been worth the risks. In any event, the shakeup provided by the war and the shocks that followed would have much to do with setting off the educational revolution which has been in progress in the quarter century since 1945.

More important than the impact of the war were the forces that were released in its aftermath. The most immediate and the most dramatic was veterans' education. The veterans' entry into the educational system was the most conspicuous aspect of the educational scene in 1945. Determined not to repeat the empty sentimentalization and practical neglect that had been offered the

8. Gordon C. Lee, "Government Pressures on the Schools During World War II," *History of Education Journal*, II (Spring 1951), pp. 65-74.

9. Francis Brown, "Colleges Gird for Total War: A Contrast with 1917-1918," *NCAQ*, XVII (April 1943), pp. 341-42.

veterans of 1918, Congress had forehandedly passed a Veterans' Readjustment Act in 1944. Public Law 346, or the "GI Bill," extended to all servicemen the benefits which had at first been offered only to disabled veterans.

No one seems to have anticipated the enthusiastic response to the educational opportunities that were offered. What began as an almost unnoticed trickle of veterans to college campuses in the months immediately following the Japanese surrender became a flood by the fall of 1946; the veterans literally crashed in the universities' doors. Enrollments shot up to the astonishing total of nearly two and a half million by 1948, or twice the 1940 figure, which had also been a record. About half the students attending college between 1946 and 1948 received veterans' benefits.

In 1947, the peak year for GI Bill enrollments, 1,122,738 veterans were registered. Nearly three million veterans were educated under the two major veterans' education laws, and the last of World War II ex-sailors and -soldiers were just leaving the campuses in 1959. Meantime, similar provisions for Korean War veterans (PL 894 and PL 550) added another 1,180,000. Altogether, about 4,000,000 veterans were educated in the colleges and universities alone at the expense of the Federal Government.[10]

Although Federal aid to education was not really new, having been given in varying forms since the young days of the Republic, it had never before been granted directly in the form of outright scholarships to students, nor had it ever been so visible nor affected so large a cross-section of the American population. The response of the veterans, and the effect upon them, was as instructive as it was unexpected. By far the largest such group the United States had ever had, they would become the most satisfactorily adjusted of all. No similar group has been less self-conscious or less demanding of recognition and compensation for past services. The successful results of the GI Bills became a powerful argument for providing Federal assistance to education in the

10. "The Federal Government and Higher Education," *Higher Education in The United States* (Washington: American Council on Education, 1961), pp. 59-60.

1960's on a comprehensive scale which would have seemed utterly unattainable only a decade earlier. (A bill to provide financial assistance to the school systems of states impoverished by the depression had been summarily rejected by Congress as recently as 1937.)

Once the dam was broken, the arguments for expanded support for education became irresistible, and states and local communities also came forward with a volume of financial support that was almost as unprecedented as the Federal assistance. From assisting the veteran and providing an essential element for national defense during the Cold War, the educational establishment would be called upon to do its share to further the cause of Civil Rights, and to help save American cities caught up in the "urban crisis." The economists added their bit by attributing a substantial percentage of the annual economic growth rate to the "development of human resources"—i.e., to education. In short, in the decades after the war Americans finally underwrote their traditional faith in free education by paying for it; heretofore its cost had been managed through inadequately equipping the schools, extracting forced subsidies from teachers in the form of inadequate salaries, begging gifts from philanthropists, and neglecting a substantial portion of the underprivileged.

The situation provided the fluidity and the breaks with tradition which reformers could seize and use. The initial postwar leap in college enrollments became permanent, except for a brief decline in the early 1950's. The physical growth of the high schools, already truly popular institutions by 1940, would be somewhat slower, but they too would share dramatically in the public interest and support as increasing numbers of their students entered the colleges, and as they felt the first impact of the social revolution which followed the war.

The accrediting agencies' immediate response was to accommodate their functions to the flood of students, hopefully with the least damage to educational standards. In the summer of 1946, the Board of Review of the NCA Commission on Colleges and Universities reminded member institutions that it was their responsibility to accept all the students they could house and teach. Concessions on faculty qualifications were permitted, provided it was understood that the concessions were strictly on an emergency basis.[11]

Resumption of the North Central Association's activities followed along lines of service and leadership that had begun to develop in the early 1930's. Temporarily diverted from this goal during the war, the Association immediately afterward continued the move away from "inspection" for the observation of fixed standards to the implementation of a new set of measures designed to encourage "quality" in whatever guise. Perhaps the most important single trend in accreditation in the years after the war was full implementation of "evaluative criteria"—as the new standards were called—in the colleges and the development of similar guidelines for high schools.

Moving beyond the specific quantitative requirements—for example, a minimum number of departments or a minimum income for a college to be acceptable—the NCA set out to achieve a kind of sophisticated sensitivity to signs of institutional quality and to develop methods of encouraging continuous improvement in the entire educational system, as much among institutions already accredited as among those striving to win their place in the ranks of the approved.

11. Editorial, *NCAQ,* XXI (July 1946), p. 2.

PART ONE

Shifting Grounds and the Beginning of Revolution
1945-1955

I

The New Emphasis on Service:
The Commission on Research and
Service

As the "inspection" aspect of accreditation was subordinated, an increasing emphasis was put upon assistance and service, upon those activities specifically undertaken by the Commission on Research and Service, and upon the continuing help rendered by the Association and its accrediting commissions. Official acknowledgement of the movement toward an enlarged emphasis upon services was made in 1942 when the Commission on Curricula of Secondary Schools and Institutions was retitled the Commission on Research and Service, its purpose being "to initiate, plan, and carry forward studies in the fields of educational and institutional research and service pertaining to universities, colleges, and secondary schools. . . ."[1]

In practice, the movement toward emphasizing service was even more marked than the new title of the Research and Service Commission indicates. The Commission on Colleges and Universities initiated many projects of its own,[2] and the Executive Com-

1. Walter J. Ziemba, "Changes in the Policies and Procedures of the Accrediting Process of the Commission on Colleges and Universities of the North Central Association of Colleges and Secondary Schools, 1909-1958" (Unpublished Ph.D. dissertation, University of Michigan, 1966), p. 253.
2. *Ibid.,* p. 250.

mittee of the Association also undertook its own studies from time to time. Indeed, the latter two tended to bypass the Research Commission so habitually that it was left in the somewhat anomalous and subordinate position of working chiefly for the Secondary Commission. Indicative of its one-sided orientation are the titles of operating subcommittees of the Research Commission, nearly every one of which was directed chiefly toward secondary school problems. Before the war there were four: the Committee on Experimental Units, the Committee on Curriculum Trends, the Committee on Functional Organization of the Secondary Schools, and the Committee on General Education in the Secondary Schools. These were reduced to three in the early 1950's: the Committee on Experimental Units, the Committee on Teacher Education, and the Committee on Current Educational Problems.

One of the early projects of the Research Commission, begun in the 1930's, was the development of experimental units for high schools; these included attempts to organize core curricula and to fuse and correlate such subjects as English and social studies. Other projects were concerned with new instructional methods and teaching materials.[3] The Committee on Experimental Units had nine unit studies, all in the social sciences, in print in 1945, and had begun the development of experimental units in arithmetic. Units published or in preparation in 1945 included *Latin America and the World Struggle for Freedom, Youth and Jobs,* and *Current Concepts in Geography.* Other units to appear in the years immediately after the war included *Atomic Energy, Conservation of Natural Resources,* and *Housing in the United States.* Most of them obviously reflected current issues. Ironically, however, a unit on *Minorities,* announced in 1946, was still in the planning stage in 1950.[4]

The most widely known and favorably received Commission

3. Davis, pp. 129-130.
4. The foregoing information on the Commission on Research and Service, unless otherwise noted, has been taken from John R. Emens, "The Activities of the Commission on Research and Service as Reflected by the Work of Its Committees," *NCAQ,* XIX (April 1945), pp. 345-355.

publication of the war years was its *General Education in the American High School*. Published in 1942 by the Committee on General Education, this report was selected by the *NEA Journal* as one of the year's outstanding books on an educational subject. A direct response to one of the liveliest issues of the day, and one that would prove to be of continuing concern, it attempted to interpret and to evaluate general education practices and to offer suggestions to improve high school programs.

However weighted its activities had been in the direction of secondary education, it was during this period that the Commission on Research and Service launched what would prove to be one of its most valuable and enduring programs for colleges. This was the Liberal Arts College Project which developed out of concern about how well liberal arts colleges were preparing secondary school teachers. In 1944 the subcommittee directing the program published *Better Colleges—Better Teachers,*[5] a study which became another widely circulated Association publication. It was in its third printing by 1947. When the original grant to support the project, $27,000 from the General Education Board, had been exhausted, a group of colleges undertook to finance it themselves. The number of participants, originally twenty-eight, was enlarged to seventy-five, and the name of the sponsoring subcommittee of the Commission was changed to the Subcommittee on Liberal Arts Education. In 1967, the group became a separate committee of the Commission with representatives on the Steering Committee.

Although it was sponsored by the NCA, a distinguishing feature of the program as it developed over the years was its spontaneity. The participants themselves determined what would be undertaken each year. The role of the NCA has been to provide a panel of coordinators/counselors, if they should be wanted, to arrange two annual four-week workshops at NCA universities

5. New York: Macmillan, 1944. For an early account of the Liberal Arts Project see Russell M. Cooper, "Working with Liberal Arts College Faculties on Teacher Education," *NCAQ,* XVI (April 1942), pp. 396-400. See also Lewis B. Mayhew, "Colleges Improve Their Programs," *Association of American Colleges Bulletin,* XLI (May 1955), pp. 284-291.

(Iowa, Michigan, Michigan State, and Minnesota have been sites), and to help with weekend intercollegiate conferences during the year.

By the early 1950's it had settled into a year-round self-study program for the participants.[6] Study projects varied widely. In the first decade not quite half were concerned with curricula or problems such as improvement of divisional organization, development of general education programs, or clarification and evaluation of institutional objectives. About a fourth of the projects dealt with improving counseling services, orienting new students, coordinating extra-curricular programs, inquiring into the reasons for student failure, and improving admissions programs. One-sixth focused on instruction itself—the improvement of classroom procedures, the use of comprehensive examinations, grading, remedial courses, audio-visual aids, reading lists, and other pertinent items. A monthly *News Bulletin* kept participants up to date on developments and findings.[7] In 1956, in response to expressed interest from some junior colleges, the study offered its services to help a group of junior colleges start a similar program of self-study and self-improvement.[8]

The project attracted considerable attention beyond the NCA territory. One of the most enduring and popular of NCA services, it came to be regarded as a model of its kind. By the mid-1950's it had evolved into a semiformalized service through which weaker institutions, to upgrade themselves, could receive assistance from the better ones, an aid program to the underdeveloped educational world, and a shining example of the Association's developing service orientation as well.[9]

6. Clarence Lee Furrow, "The North Central Liberal Arts Study," *NCAQ*, XXV (April 1951), pp. 361-63.

7. Anna Caroline Greve, "Practices and Procedures Developed in the North Central Association Study for the Improvement of Liberal Arts Education," (Ph.D. dissertation, University of Minnesota, 1950), pp. 170-173. See also Lewis B. Mayhew, "Interinstitutional Cooperation through Regional Studies," *Higher Education,* XI (March 1955), pp. 103-105.

8. Lewis B. Mayhew, "Report of the Committee on Liberal Arts Education," *NCAQ*, XXXII (April 1958), p. 289.

9. Mayhew, "Interinstitutional Cooperation etc.," p. 103; Mayhew, "Report etc.," p. 290.

A similar program for eighteen teachers colleges was initiated in 1947. (There were seventy-five teachers colleges in the NCA area at the time.) In 1956 the subcommittee in charge published a comprehensive book-length report on its activities.[10] Like the Liberal Arts Project, this program proceeded from the view that the best way to produce good teachers was to improve the colleges they attended. A vital service of the Teacher Education Project has been the visit of a mature faculty member or administrator to each participating campus once a year. The visitor has provided stimulus for institutional self-study. The Project also has encouraged an exchange plan in which a college plays host to a delegation of eight to ten faculty members from another institution.

The Project has scheduled an annual four-week workshop for faculty members from participating colleges. Held on the campus of the University of Minnesota, the workshop has had the assistance of the University's facilities.

By the mid-1950's the teachers and liberal arts college projects were in close communication, a development furthered by their sharing the *News Bulletin*. Although efforts were made to develop a similar program in the large universities, they met with little success.

The recognition of the decreasing areas of difference between the private liberal arts colleges and the public teachers colleges reflected a significant change taking place in higher education, one the NCA furthered by emphasizing general education in all colleges, whatever their purposes, as the essential core of good teacher preparation. An unremarked side effect of these college improvement programs was that they probably did as much or more to "articulate" high school and college work as any of the more self-conscious efforts that were brought forward from time to time. (One of the recurring issues in the period was the need to develop closer cooperation between schools and colleges; it produced more committees than concrete results.)

10. George E. Hill and E. E. Potthoff (eds.), *Improving Teacher Education Through Inter-college Cooperation* (Dubuque, Iowa: Wm. C. Brown Co., 1956).

A related concern was the improvement of teachers already in the schools. An In-service Education for Teachers Subcommittee of the Research and Service Commission was formed in 1943 to develop a body of procedures for the schools. In 1953 it distributed a pamphlet entitled "Incentives Used in Motivation of the Professional Growth of Teachers," which was followed a year later by a thirty-five page guide for setting up teacher improvement workshops in the schools. The subcommittee also organized discussion group meetings on the general topic of in-service teacher improvement at the annual NCA meetings.[11]

Indeed, teacher education, or the improvement of teaching, absorbed the attention of no fewer than half the fourteen projects of the Commission on Research and Service in the middle 1950's.[12] Other projects included a report with recommendations on guidance and counseling in the high schools,[13] an extensive investigation, begun in 1952, of school libraries and the training of librarians; another on reading improvement, begun in 1954;[14] and another on student practice teaching.

The library study, which was completed in 1954, revealed that only one state, Illinois, had higher requirements for high school librarians than those set by the NCA. Most schools were employing librarians with little or no professional training for their jobs. The final report of the committee recommended strong measures for improvement, particularly in professional training for librarians in accredited schools. Twenty-four semester credits in professional courses—the same number required for teaching a high school subject—was established as an ideal minimum, although it

11. James R. Mitchell, "The Workshop as an In-Service Education Procedure," *NCAQ*, XXIX (April 1954), pp. 421-457; W. Fred Totten, "Research and Service Needed by Both the Commission on Colleges and Universities and the Commission on Secondary Schools," *NCAQ*, XXIX (October 1954).

12. Organization Chart, November 1955; Cooper, "North Central Activities in Teacher Education," *NCAQ*, XXXIII (April 1959), p. 286.

13. See Subcommittee on Guidance of the Committee on Current Educational Problems, "Extended or Potential Optimum Guidance Practices in Small, Medium, and Large North Central High Schools, 1948-49." *NCAQ*, XXIV (October 1949), pp. 174-246.

14. "Improvement of Reading in Colleges and Secondary Schools," *NCAQ*, XXXI (October 1956), pp. 199-208.

was generally recognized that in practice the requirement could be imposed only gradually and would have to be graduated downward for small schools. (Trained librarians were in short supply; six of the nineteen NCA states had no colleges or universities offering as much as twenty-four hours of study in library science.)

Four hundred dollars per year was recommended as a minimum expenditure for schools with fewer than two hundred pupils and $1.50 per pupil for those enrolling more than five hundred, a modest proposal which indicated clearly the need for improvement in school libraries. The study deserves special notice as an example of a commissioned study to determine what was both desirable and feasible as a standard for accreditation. It also demonstrated how regional associations did on occasion make use of what was being done elsewhere; in this instance the NCA profited from and built upon the earlier experience of the Southern Association and its detailed requirements for school libraries.[15]

All of the programs mentioned thus far enjoyed a considerable measure of success. On the other hand, the Association effort to influence the content and direction of secondary education directly through its Committee on Experimental Units never fulfilled the original expectations. When the experimental unit progam was launched in 1937, there was some hope that it would develop into a vehicle for curricular reform and hopefully into a major publishing enterprise and a source of revenue for the Association. After years of effort only nine experimental unit titles were in print. Sales were slow; although a million copies of units were distributed between 1948 and 1954, sales had dropped to only 40,000 in the latter year, about enough to keep the enterprise going, but not enough to attract a commercial publisher or to be a major influence.[16]

15. Report of School-Library Study Committee to the Steering Committee of the Research and Service Commission, June 24, 1954; Charles E. Hood, "The Library Study of the North Central Association," *Proceedings, Northwest Association of Secondary and Higher Schools,* 1954, p. 58.

16. Maurice L. Hartung, "The Role of the North Central Association Units in the Social Studies Program," *NCAQ,* XVII (October 1942). pp. 200-201;

By one of those strange ironies, however, the very report which gloomily confessed accomplishments considerably short of the original expectations also contained an announcement of yet another experimental unit program which would turn out to be an unqualified success. A newly formed Subcommittee on Foreign Affairs had been authorized to seek funds, in cooperation with Science Research Associates, from the Ford Foundation to develop materials on foreign affairs and international relations for high schools.

The project was in response, first of all, to considerable criticism of the public schools for neglecting the study of foreign relations at a time when the United States was involved in the prolonged Cold War and had just emerged from the Korean conflict. Almost equally important was the decision to determine whether the experimental unit program could be salvaged if a massive effort were made to put new life into its publications. Adequate financial support, a two-year experimental pilot program, extensive promotion by mail and in regional conferences, and vigorous distribution of materials, all were to be combined to "determine whether . . . a really significant addition and contribution [could] be effectively accomplished in the high schools of America."[17]

In 1956, the Ford Foundation awarded $125,000 for the pilot program, and James Becker, assistant professor of social studies at Illinois Normal University, was appointed to direct the project. It began with a number of unit-bulletins on current foreign problems prepared by academic scholars. For example, Henry Roberts and Paul Zinner of Columbia University were persuaded to collaborate on a unit on the United States and Russian Relations, and Harold Deutsch of the University of Minnesota agreed to develop a suitable study on the relations of the United States and Germany. In format, content, and style the booklets were in-

---

J. E. Stonecipher, "The Publication of Experimental Unit Studies as an Educational Source," *NCAQ*, XX (October 1945), pp. 158-161.

17. Editorial, *NCAQ*, XXX (April 1956), pp. 312-314; James M. Becker, "NCA Foreign Relations Project," *Social Education*, XXI (November 1957), pp. 316-318; *Ibid.*, XXIII (October 1959), pp. 274-76.

tended to "bridge the gap between the text and the weeklies. . . ."[18]

Eighteen mid-western high schools selected for a pilot program were closely supervised by the staff of the project; a control group of nine other high schools used the materials without outside direction. The tryout was an instantaneous success, and in 1957 the Ford Foundation renewed its support with a grant of $250,000. In the second year, following a series of workshops to evaluate and suggest revisions of the materials, five hundred schools entered the program.[19] The project soon became firmly established as the most useful and popular addition the Committee on Experimental Units had ever contributed to the high school curriculum.

The most timely responses to contemporary issues were the study projects undertaken by the Research Commission's Committee on Current Educational Problems. A Subcommittee on High School-College Relations was formed in 1949, one on Social Experiences and Organizations in 1950 (to study the impact of the fraternity movement in high schools), another in 1953 to study and report on the educational possibilities of television, and another in 1954 to make recommendations for reading improvement programs in high schools and colleges.

Articulation of high school and college curricula and procedures was a problem as old as the Association; it had, indeed, been the main reason for its founding. The considerable number of experiments and proposals put forward by national organizations, by state education departments, or by cooperative groups of colleges and high schools was clear evidence that a satisfactory answer was as elusive as it was desired. Although the Liberal Arts and Teacher Education Projects could be considered steps toward articulation, such a development as the growing tendency of colleges to use entrance examinations was a step in the opposite direction. A preliminary report authorized by the NCA Executive Committee in 1949 summarized the history of the problem and the issues involved. The next year the Research and Ser-

18. Editorial, *NCAQ*, XXX (April 1956), pp. 312-314.
19. *Ibid.*

vice Commission appointed a Subcommittee on Articulation of High Schools and Colleges. Although detailed plans for proceeding were suggested, not so much as a clear identification of what the problem actually was had been achieved by 1955, when the subcommittee was continued for one more year.[20]

Television's great promise for education was already generally acknowledged when the first Television Committee was formed in 1953. Moreover, educational television was already a fact. In 1950 two NCA members, Iowa State College and Western Reserve University, became the first educational institutions to own TV stations and the first to offer TV courses for credit. Seven years later, sixteen such TV stations were in operation in NCA territory, two more were under construction, construction permits were issued for five more, three had applications on file, and one application was pending—twenty-seven altogether in varying stages of development in the nineteen NCA states.

In early 1955, the Television Committee published a general statement entitled "Promise and Philosophy," which declared that television was "an opportunity for all education and a challenge to the profession. . . ." The committee also announced that it would set itself to the task of disseminating information about educational television, encouraging exploration and evaluation of the medium by schools in the NCA area, and recommending accreditation standards to the NCA Executive Board.

The impact of television was bound to be large in a situation in which rising expenses, climbing enrollments, and teacher shortages were forcing institutions to look beyond the conventional solutions to such problems. In the absence of any clear voice of leadership from any other quarter, the NCA was in an unusually advantageous position to take the lead itself. In the next decade the Association played a significant role in encouraging the establishment of Educational-TV stations as well as the use of closed-circuit TV for college courses and teacher education, and

20. Manning M. Pattillo and Lorence Stout, "Co-operation between Secondary Schools and Colleges," *NCAQ*, XXV (January 1951), pp. 313-343.

in furthering the development of new courses designed for the new communications medium.

Three new subcommittees to consider reading problems in high schools and colleges (1954), education of the superior and talented student (1955), and the improvement of human relations in the classroom (1956) were directly related to the rising tensions of the 1950's and to the growing conviction that education which was almost the same for everyone—long a cherished ideal —was inadequate for a large number of students in any institution. With American education through college becoming a part of the "rising expectations" of hitherto neglected elements of the population, such matters as inadequate reading skills had intruded into the high schools and colleges.

Studies of the reading and learning processes as well as sharpened social awareness put the schools and their representatives into the position of having to accept responsibility for improvement, instead of permitting them to write off poor readers as unintelligent and therefore to be excluded from the higher levels of education. On the other end of the scale, equal attention was directed to the plight of the ultra-privileged superior student bound to a grade level and a mass-oriented curriculum that failed to interest or challenge him. The appearance of the two committees to recommend adjustment to extreme variations in student bodies was a move toward the practical application of the principle of flexibility and variety that was being developed in the Association's approach to accreditation.

The Committee on Human Relations in the Classroom reflected the rising national concern about racial and cultural discrimination. It was the first truly open acknowledgement by the Association that the problem required more from the organization than the mere adjustment to whatever the social climate dictated. One of the curious anomalies of American education has been the general acceptance of responsibility for teaching morals and American ideals as well as a considerable reformist bent among some of its leaders, and at the same time the acceptance, if not outright approval, of the prevailing policy on the Negro. From the mid-1950's the schools and colleges would become both the forums and battle grounds for debating and resolving great public issues that agitated the nation. The Committee on Human Relations, formed in 1956, promised an important step in the extension of the services of the Association, and in addition a broadening of the conception of accreditation.

II

Policies and Trends in Accreditation, 1945-1955: Accommodating to Change

When the war ended the Commission on Colleges and Universities was already well along in its second generation of accreditation, which dated from 1934 when a committee of Association leaders had recommended dropping quantitative standards in favor of a new approach which would emphasize the less easily quantified concept of "quality." The old standards and procedures were said to be overly formal and arbitrary, unfit to strike a balance between the strengths and weaknesses of institutions or to accommodate to the unique and special aims of an institution.[1] The guiding principles for accreditation adopted by the committee in 1934 were that

1. A standard should not be regarded as fixed but as referring to something alive and developing.
2. A standard should be an induction, something to proceed from.
3. The North Central Association should be less a judge and more a creator.
4. The North Central standards should be statements of policy, not the framework or skeleton outline of a scheme.
5. The standards of the North Central Association should be

1. Davis, pp. 69-70. The committee report was completed in 1934, but was not published until 1936.

such that a school would know whether it was improving and measuring up to reasonable conditions.[2]

The report, which was adopted by the Association in April 1934, recommended the replacement of specific standards by

> . . . the total pattern . . . as an institution of higher education. While institutions will be judged in terms of the characteristics noted in this statement of policy, it is recognized that wide variations will appear in the degree of excellence attained. It is accepted as a principle of procedure that superiority in some characteristics may be regarded as compensating, to some extent, for deficiencies in other respects. The facilities and activities of an institution will be judged in terms of the purposes it seeks to serve.[3]

In short, the primary purpose of the program was "to inaugurate a plan that would stimulate continuous growth toward ideals of educational quality. . . ."

The Commission on Secondary Schools soon followed with proposals for a similar study, which developed into the much broader National Cooperative Study, drawing personnel and suggestions from a number of academic and accrediting bodies. In due time evaluation standards for secondary schools also shifted in the direction of an assessment of the "total pattern" of a school. A general report of the National Cooperative Study was published in 1939, and the first edition of the *Evaluative Criteria* appeared in 1940. Revisions were scheduled every ten years—the second appeared on schedule in 1950 and the third in 1960.[4]

To be sure, the old quantitative standards were altered only gradually, in part because a great many examiners were more comfortable with concrete measures than only partially defined ideals. Nevertheless, there had been introduced a revolutionary principle that a community might have a legitimate purpose for its school which did not necessarily conform to a general regional

2. As reported by Lotus Coffman, President of the University of Minnesota, who chaired the committee.

3. Quoted in Davis, p. 72.

4. George E. Carrothers, "Early Beginnings of the Cooperative Study of Secondary School Standards," *NCAQ*, XXIX (October 1954), pp. 178-184.

consensus. (It was not foreseen, of course, that in the late 1960's the principle of uniqueness and special purposes could be translated into neighborhood control as a measure to further or to frustrate civil rights reform.)

A. The Commission on Colleges and Universities

Indicative of the spirit of the NCA reforms in college requirements following the Cooperative Committee report of 1934 was the changed language associated with accreditation. "Inspection" gave way to "evaluation," "standard" was used with decreasing frequency, and such words as "criteria," "ideals," "growth," "objectives," and "individuality " were conspicuous. A new principle of "individuality of institution" was given a prominent place; uniformity was even marked down as undesirable, and experimentation was to be "encouraged." A "pattern map" made of each institution was to show how it compared on any selected characteristic with other accredited institutions.

A manual outlining policies and procedures published in 1934 provided details for the new approach to accreditation. It was revised in 1938 chiefly to incorporate changes indicated after four years of experience. Among the more important recommendations was one to curb the growth of proprietary bodies by defining an educational institution as "a non-profit corporation devoted primarily to educational purposes." A change in an institution's major purposes was now given as grounds for a full-reevaluation, and the requirement that purposes and practices must be in agreement was strengthened. Faculty acceptance of an institution's stated purposes was declared to be essential in the 1938 revision. The new manual also described in some detail the necessity for administrators to consult faculty and to resist pressures from governing boards or from "outside" when recruiting faculty.

The same liberalizing tendencies and concern for institutional integrity and independence encouraged revisions in curriculum. Definitions of acceptable professional and technical education were broadened to cover seventeen different kinds of schools—only two had qualified under the earlier rules. Requirements on curriculum, library, and financial responsibility were loosened to almost no specific limitations at all. But considerable emphasis was placed upon an institution's living up to its own declared ideals and upon its continuing improvement.

It was this modified manual, with a few minor changes added in 1941, in which the NCA set out to be an encouraging and understanding assistant, that would serve as the NCA guide to accreditation until the mid-1950's. Indeed, the major revision then undertaken was less a change to a new approach than an attempt to implement institutional evaluation in terms of quality, uniqueness, and community service.[1] The only important changes introduced in 1941 were separate procedures for evaluating junior colleges. A final modification, published in 1954, sharply cut the text of the manual, and went even further from specific requirements in the direction of variation and flexibility. Even the requirement of a satisfactory general education program, historically the core of the NCA definition of an acceptable collegiate offering, was altered to permit a wide range of variation in line with an institution's specific role.

One of the immediate results of the revisions was a reduction in the number of detailed forms to be filled out. These were further reduced during the war and reduced even more when four of the stalwart members of the NCA, all Big Ten Universities, objected to the repetitiveness of the biennial reports required on faculty qualifications, and briefly boycotted them.[2]

Change was also reflected in a revision of the "inspection" procedure, which now became an "examination." In the first years after the new approach was adopted several studies and

1. Norman Burns, "Some Thoughts on the Theory and Practice of Accrediting," *NCAQ*, XXVII (October 1953), pp. 205-217. Burns, then secretary of the Commission on Colleges and Universities, argued that there had continued to be far too much of judging "quality" by quantitative standards. See also Burns, "Accrediting: Its Response to an Evolving System of Higher Education," in James Fisher and David Sweet (eds.), *Problems and Prospects in Higher Education* (Manuscript to be published 1970).

2. Ziemba, pp. 143-172, 188.

practice visits were conducted in order to test its effectiveness and to establish measurements of what to expect. The first trial run was a survey of the YMCA College in Chicago by a team of NCA notables. A provision adopted in 1940 specified that at least one examiner on a survey team should be from the type of institution under examination. That same year separate report forms were devised for (a) two-year institutions, (b) four-year colleges, (c) master's degree-granting institutions, and (d) complex universities offering doctorates and professional degrees.[3] All were significant steps in the movement away from a single standard for higher education.

However, these procedures applied only to institutions seeking initial accreditation, that is, to the newest and presumably the weakest ones. Once an institution was accredited, it was required only to submit certain biennial reports, on different aspects of its operation each time. As a result, until 1957, when a new program of periodic review visits for all NCA institutions was begun, some institutions escaped any really close scrutiny year after year if they did not draw attention to themselves by a flagrant violation of Association standards.

The virtue of the system was that accredited institutions were almost entirely autonomous as long as they maintained a minimal standard of performance. On the other hand, the Association offered few incentives for upgrading institutions beyond the minimal standards it set for entry. Such pressures for improvement that might affect NCA institutions were more likely to come from their own faculty and administrations, from inter-institutional rivalry, or from the pride of a constituency than from official action of the Association.

A serious problem under the revised procedures was the shortage of qualified examiners. The work of examination had become considerably more exacting because so much depended upon the examiner's experience, acumen, and judgment. A major obstacle

3. Ziemba, pp. 201-206. See also "Summary of Procedures Used in Verifying and Revising the Classification of Member Institutions, June 1946." (Mimeographed circular.)

to the effective implementation of the qualitative approach was the fact that it was much easier and more reassuring for an examiner to count the number of Ph.D's on a faculty than it was to measure its collective teaching effectiveness. The manuals issued for the guidance of examiners after 1934 (no manual had been provided for inspectors before that date), advised examining teams to talk over the implication of data submitted with administrative officers and members of the faculty before the official examination. Examiners were urged to gather whatever additional information seemed necessary through personal observation and conferences. A list of directions for the examiners further specified details of what they were to do in order to perform as well as possible a task that was constantly requiring more and more expert knowledge and experience.

A simple measure of the growing complexity of accreditation procedures is their increasing costs. In the early 1920's a full survey cost an institution only $25. Costs rose rapidly after the late 1920's and in 1946 a degree-granting institution was charged $500 for a survey. A decade later it was set at $300 per examiner plus a $500 institutional fee.[4]

Accreditation policy on junior colleges and graduate education assumed great importance in the post-war era—and added to the burden of examination. A steep climb in graduate enrollment was matched by a rapid rise in the number of junior and community colleges. The increase in the number of institutions offering graduate programs was partially in response to the Secondary Commission's raising preparation requirements for teachers in secondary schools. From the early 1940's the Commission's Criteria 6 and 7 for secondary schools stated that:

> . . . The secondary school (must be) under the direction of a well-trained and competent school administrator who possesses as a minimum a Master's degree from an institution of higher education accredited by the North Central

4. Ziemba, pp. 212-221. The manuals continued unchanged from 1934 to 1954. In 1948 the Board of Review was empowered to weed out the prospects which had no chance of accreditation, which both saved the institutions the expense of a survey and conserved the time of the limited number of expert examiners available to the Association.

Association . . . or by one of the other regional accrediting associations. . . .

. . . In evaluating the adequacy of the general preparation of the instructional and supervisory staff, State Committees will take into consideration the extent to which the staff as a whole has completed work beyond the Bachelor's degree, also the kind and distribution of college courses taken and the recency of their completion.[5]

The question of what to do about the expansion of offerings also raised issues of jurisdiction and prior claims. Certain established institutions, e.g., the universities, had long regarded graduate education as their own special province; moreover, they and the Commission on Colleges and Universities were deeply concerned about the level and quality of programs that aspiring colleges all too frequently drew up hastily with little real preparation. A rule-of-thumb policy dating from before the war provided little effective control. It simply "required" that institutions offering the M.A. should rank in the sixtieth percentile in criteria significant for graduate study, and those offering the doctorate in the eightieth. Institutions that fell below these levels were not to be approved without a full on-site survey by the Association. Not infrequently the requirement was ignored—if it were even known —and institutions simply went ahead with new programs without informing anyone.[6]

A major step toward establishing a full accreditation procedure for graduate programs was made in 1948 when the Commission announced that accredited institutions contemplating adding M.A. and Ph.D. programs must first submit a series of special reports and obtain the approval of the Board of Review and the Association secretary. Following preliminary approval, the institution could begin; after one year a committee from the NCA would visit the institution to determine whether final approval was warranted.[7]

5. Quoted in *NCAQ*, XIX (July 1944), p. 39.
6. See *NCAQ*, XXIV (July 1949), p. 10.
7. At its annual meeting in December 1946, the Southern Association instructed its Commission on Higher Education to formulate standards and procedures for the accreditation of graduate programs. The Commission

In 1950 the procedure was further revised to fit graduate accreditation into the ideal of evaluating institutions in terms of their success in achieving their own stated purposes. On the ground that when institutions expanded into graduate programs they had in fact significantly altered their character, the Association decided that any such expansion would be approved only after a full accreditation survey of the applying institution's entire operation.

A new "Procedure for Accreditation of Graduate Programs" prescribed the following steps: (1) a full self-survey report filed with the secretary of the Commission on Colleges and Universities; (2) a Board of Review advisory opinion to the applying institution following a study of the self-survey; and (3) following the inauguration of a new program, a full survey by an Association team using the same procedures applicable to any institution applying for inital accreditation.

The one-year grace period before evaluation that was first permitted was extended in 1955 to whatever date the first student in a new program was graduated. The procedure was not applied to institutions with already accredited Master's or Doctoral programs which were simply being extended or enriched. These institutions were merely required to report their plans on a brief form provided by the Commission on Colleges and Universities. In short, the NCA policies on graduate accreditation consisted more or less of seeing that accepted standards prevalent at the universities were followed by newcomers.

On the other end of the higher education system a real opportunity for innovation was developing in the junior and community colleges. Here no establishment or tradition existed. In its earliest ventures in junior college accreditation, the NCA had assigned two-year colleges to the jurisdiction of the Higher Commission. Some confusion arose in dealing with four-year institutions which combined the last two years of high school with the first two of college. Until 1941 this issue was solved by giving

---

report, which was published in 1948, was a detailed guide much like the standard graduate school entry in a university catalog. *The Southern Association Quarterly*, XII (February 1948), pp. 222-235.

the accrediting commissions responsibility for the parts of such four-year programs that fell within their province. The solution did not appear satisfactory to everyone, either in the NCA or in the institutions affected, with the result that a good many of them did not bother with accreditation.[8] (The Council of North Central Junior Colleges was established at this time independent of the NCA.)

In 1941 a conference committee of three representatives from the commissions attempted to develop a more suitable procedure. Junior colleges were to be classified as: Type I, two-year institutions operating on a strictly collegiate basis; and Type II, institutions which were half high school and half college. The College Commission was assigned undivided jurisdiction in accrediting Type I. Type II institutions were to be recognized as unique institutions and were to be placed under a special committee of one representative each from the accrediting commissions and one selected by accredited junior colleges. This committee was instructed to devise a set of suitable standards by combining the Higher Commission schedules and secondary school criteria.[9] The significant aspect of the proposal was the assumption that Type II schools were something new that had to be assessed on a new set of criteria.

Although the recommendation for a special committee was approved by the Secondary Commission's Administrative Committee in 1943, the development of suitable measures for junior colleges progressed slowly. In 1945 the Association ruled that such institutions would be handled as single units, with special reports required from those which were part of a public school system. All applications were to be made to the secretary of the Association, and examining committees were to consist of one member named by the Higher Commission and one by the Secondary Commission. Their reports and recommendations were to be acted upon by the executive bodies of the two commissions meeting in joint session. Accredited institutions were to be listed on both

8. Fewer than half the junior colleges in the NCA area were accredited in 1941.
9. Report of Conference Committee on Junior College Accreditation, 1941.

commissions' lists. Again, progress was slow, and the situation in the other regional associations appears to have been little if any better. Of the 662 junior colleges listed in the 1948 *Directory* of the American Association of Junior Colleges, only 171 were accredited by regional associations.[10]

In his annual report to the Higher Commission in 1948, Secretary Norman Burns called particular attention to the need and opportunity to do something for junior colleges. He announced that the two accrediting commissions' governing committees were recommending that yet another committee be formed to study the junior college situation with the intention of establishing appropriate accreditation measurements. The study began that same year with 155 junior colleges in the NCA area agreeing to participate.[11] The committee was still without a solution as late as 1952, and procedure for applications remained the same as they had in 1945. In 1960 the American Council on Education report on junior colleges observed that the regional associations were still applying largely quantitative measurements to these institutions and had failed to arrive at any satisfactory standards for them.[12]

One of the ironies of an extremely active transitional period in the history of the Association was the amount of time given to trying to reform intercollegiate athletic practices. The problem was simple enough and well understood: the undercover professionalization and overemphasis of competitive sports rationalized in pious rhetoric about character building and Americanism. Since high schools were affected both by the example of the universities and by the various devices and subterfuges to recruit their star athletes, both of the accrediting commissions were concerned and found here one of their rare opportunities to attack an issue together.

General awareness of the problem dated from the 1930's or earlier when athletic scholarships came to full flower. The NCA held its first conference on athletics in 1932, and first proposed

10. *NCAQ*, XIX (October 1945), p. 192; *The American Junior College* (Washington: American Council on Education, 1960), p. 24.
11. *NCAQ*, XXIII (July 1948), pp. 19-20; XXIV (July 1949), p. 9.
12. *The American Junior College*, p. 25.

minimum standards for intercollegiate athletics in 1933. However, it was not until 1941, when the revised manual on accrediting included a section on athletics, that the NCA officially announced its active concern.[13] Three years later the Board of Review of the Commission on Colleges and Universities noted the tendency for collegiate institutions to enter upon "extended programs of intercollegiate athletics in a manner which seems to jeopardize the soundness of their academic services." It urged that the section on athletics in the Revised Manual on Accrediting be brought individually to the attention of college presidents.

Meanwhile, professionalization and shading of ethical standards were exemplified in such athletic scandals of the late 1940's as the West Point football affair, an upheaval at William and Mary College, and the indictments of college basketball players for accepting bribes.[14] In the summer of 1951, following complaints from the Commission on Secondary Schools, the Executive Committee of the Association appointed a special Intercollegiate and Interscholastic Athletic Committee to advise it on correcting the situation in *both* college and high school athletics.

The subsequent committee report condemned lax admissions standards for athletes, unscrupulous recruiting, and athletic scholarships. A new code of regulations followed and was unanimously approved at the annual meeting of the Association in 1952.[15] The Secondary Commission meanwhile adopted its own regulations to control the high schools' relations with college athletic departments. A bold move, it was the most vigorous effort ever undertaken by an accrediting association to return athletic activities to their proper role of no more nor less than an integral part of an educational program.

The first step toward getting the job done was the formation of the Committee on Athletic Problems to oversee the work and to

13. J. B. Edmonson, "The New Athletic Regulations," *NCAQ*, XXVIII (January 1953), p. 297.

14. *NCAQ*, XXVI (October 1951), p. 157; Johnson, "Intercollegiate Athletics etc.," pp. 180-181; see also contemporary newspapers.

15. Edmonson, "New Athletic Regulations," pp. 297-98; Manning Pattillo, "Athletics in Some of the Better Colleges and Universities," *NCAQ* (April 1953), p. 332.

persuade the colleges and universities to comply. Had this committee and its predecessor had their way, intercollegiate athletics today would be entirely different from what they are. What was intended is clearly indicated in several articles published in the *Quarterly* which described the de-emphasized athletics programs at such prestigious colleges and universities as Chicago, Johns Hopkins, Haverford, Amherst, Swarthmore, Harvard, and Oberlin. Manning Pattillo, the recently appointed associate secretary of the Commission, introduced the articles with some pointed comments on "the destructive tradition of athletics as business enterprise and public entertainment. . . ."

The *Quarterly* also published a report on athlete recruitment in the high schools. The text and tables of this survey contained the unhappy facts of the situation as viewed by many high school administrators and teachers: easy college admissions and even lucrative scholarships for young athletes barely able to get through high school on the one hand, and open marketing of their products by high school coaches and "quarterback" groups on the other.[16]

The National Collegiate Athletic Association promptly retaliated by announcing that athletics was outside the jurisdiction of the NCA or any other regional association. Somewhat more surprising was the attitude taken by some of the leading university members of the Association. When two of them were threatened with disaccreditation at the annual meeting of 1953, the opposition came to a head. On April 27 representatives of twenty-seven institutions, nine of which had representatives on the Commission on Colleges and Universities which had adopted the regulations, met in Chicago and discussed the situation with the Commission's executive secretary, Norman Burns. They then approved and released to the press a statement demanding that the NCA drop its prohibition of athletic scholarships. Rumors also went around, very likely let out deliberately, that some of the larger universities were contemplating withdrawal from the Association. Indeed, some did threaten privately to do so.[17]

16. Edmonson, p. 299; Otto Hughes, "The Recruitment of Athletes," *NCAQ,* XXVIII (October 1953), pp. 218-228.
17. J. B. Edmonson and Eugene Youngert, "Report to the Commission of

On June 12, the Board of Review of the Commission on Colleges and Universities met in special session with the "twenty-seven" who represented most of the major athletic conferences of the region. The chief point at issue was subsidization, and while the cold minutes of the session do not reveal much about the emotional tone of the discussions, some indications of heat do appear. The spokesmen for the chief complainants, the Big Ten universities, professed to see little harm in giving subsidies to athletes and more than a little good in "entertainment" athletics. Representatives of the smaller institutions of the Rocky Mountain area and of municipal universities, on the other hand, sharply criticized the entire structure and rationalization of "semi-professional" intercollegiate athletics.

In the end the big institutions had their way, and the conference recommended that the NCA policy be modified to conform to the American Council on Education recommendation on the matter of subsidization, namely that "Athletes holding scholarships or grants-in-aid should be required to meet the same standards of academic performance and economic need as are required of all other recipients," pending a study and a restatement of policy to be submitted to referendum by the institution membership.[18]

One more committee, of eight members, two of whom were high school representatives, others being university and college administrators, was appointed to replace the original committee.[19] The athletic policy it worked out for the Association was the expected surrender:

> Institutions of higher education will be expected to conduct their intercollegiate athletic programs in a fashion consistent with the overall educational objectives of each campus. . . . However, the North Central Association does not abrogate its right to make any investigations of inter-

[sic] Colleges and of [sic] Universities, On Athletics," 1954; see also, Minutes, Special Joint Meeting, Executive Committee, NCA, and Board of Review, Commission on Colleges and Universities, May 21, 1953.

18. Minutes, Special Meeting, Board of Review, Commission on Colleges and Universities, June 1953, pp. 1-2.

19. Edmonson and Youngert, "Report etc."

collegiate athletic policies or practices in higher institutions which it feels are necessary or desirable, and to take appropriate action as a consequence of its investigations.[20]

It was unaltered a decade later.

Yet the advocates of reform were not without strong support. Several university presidents, whose foothall teams were nationally famous, apparently saw a chance to get out of an increasingly expensive and embarrassing situation and to recover control of an athletic department that had become semi-autonomous in the university structure. Also, the NCA had strong support from its high school membership, who had had more than enough of university recruiters badgering their athletes and working directly with coaches and local boosters behind the backs of faculties and administrations. In fact, it had been a high school principal who had brought the complaint that had started the whole thing, and it had been the Commission on Secondary Schools which had made the initial recommendation for an investigation to the Association.[21]

Had the Association, and in particular the Commission on Colleges and Universities, been strong enough to control the large universities, the outcome would have been different. Turning as it did around recruitment, as well as subsidization, the athletics issue was clearly an Association-wide problem, an opportunity to develop some "articulation" of policy between high school and university. Indeed, a few moves did originate from the athletic committees and the Higher Commission secretarial office to develop a broad base of support among college and high school faculties and even among their lay supporters, but these came to nothing.[22] The university administrations were not interested; their failure to consider how their policies affected anyone but themselves did little to improve the relationship between the two branches of education represented by the Association.

20. Minutes, Executive Board, Commission on Colleges and Universities, June 1957.
21. Edmonson, "New Athletic Regulations," pp. 297-302; Hughes, "Recruitment of Athletes," pp. 218-228.
22. Report, Sixth Conference of State Chairmen, Commission on Secondary Schools, NCA, October 1-2, 1952.

B. The Commission on Secondary Schools

A significant aspect of the process of secondary school accreditation has always been the decentralized, state-level procedure, conducted by a State Committee of principals and superintendents which is headed by a chairman who is either appointed from the state university's college of education or is a member of the state department of secondary education. By contrast, the first move to any sort of decentralization in the Higher Commission's operation would not come until its reorganization in 1956, when "Committees by Type" and regional groups were set up. The local character of the secondary accreditation process was the chief factor in the direct and sometimes dramatic way in which it worked. It was in the deliberations of this Commission that one could find the open fight, and it was this Commission that did not shrink from dropping from membership school systems as highly regarded as those of Chicago and Kansas City. The Higher Commission would undoubtedly encounter difficulty in attempting the same with a large well-established university.

In spite of the grass roots orientation of the Secondary Commission and in spite of some moves to draw teachers into its survey teams, it continued to be dominated by principals, superintendents, and education professors; in the Higher Commission the role of the academicians—the "subject matter" people —was being expanded, almost but not quite into the highest level of deliberation. The contrast was, of course, a reflection of the considerable differences between secondary schools and universities in faculty-administration relationships. Even at the end of the 1960's the schools were still some distance from fully accepting faculty participation in decision-making as a matter of general policy. Academic freedom in the schools was yet in its early stages, and often not fully understood by teachers, administrators, or boards of education. Here, especially, was one of the widest gaps between outlook and situation of the college and the high school.

A general trend toward broadening participation in the NCA by representatives of the schools, which had already started before the war when state committees were enlarged, moved forward rapidly after the conflict ended. In 1948 the Secondary Commission required that these committees include a secondary school specialist nominated from his faculty by the president of the state university; the director of secondary education in the state department of education or a member nominated by the State Superintendent of Public Instruction; and three to five principals of accredited secondary schools, depending upon the number in a state. Reviewing committees were also enlarged.

Annual meetings of high school principals sponsored by State Committees which began in 1947, increasingly opened their sessions to the public in order to popularize and explain the work of the Association. The New Mexico State Committee went even further by holding annual meetings at various locations in order to explain the rules and procedures of the Association to its member schools.[1] Such meetings also were moving toward formulating and suggesting general policies for the Commission, a really significant step in the direction of member participation for which there was no real counterpart in the Commission on Colleges and Universities.

The key figure in the state committees was the state chairman; in most cases, he was a member of the professional education faculty at the state university. The chairman necessarily did most of the work of collecting and filing reports, and executing directives from the Commission. What this meant in practice, of course, was that state university colleges of education had a large role in high school accreditation. In other words, grass roots participation had its limitations.

Although the Secondary Commission would be confronted with problems on every hand, some of them postponed from before the war emergency, and some produced by the war and its aftermath, perhaps the most fundamental task before it was to make ef-

1. Nelson L. Haggerson, "The North Central Association at the Grass Roots in New Mexico," *NCAQ*, XXXII (April 1958), pp. 335-337.

fective use of the *Evaluative Criteria* developed by the Cooperative Study of Secondary School Standards in 1940 and revised in 1950.[2] Some influential members of the Commission insisted that the *Evaluative Criteria* be incorporated without further delay into the NCA standards and procedures for secondary schools. These vehement advocates charged that the Association leadership had been shockingly remiss about revising the high school criteria.

Indeed, acceptance of the new standards had proceeded somewhat more slowly within the NCA, despite its leadership in initiating the Cooperative Study, than in some of the other regional associations. By the end of the 1946 school year, only 401 of the 3,031 NCA secondary schools had been officially reevaluated. Seventy-four other member schools completed a self-evaluation using one or more sections of the *Evaluative Criteria*. This was the lowest figure for any of the regional associations; the Middle States Association had reevaluated nearly 70 per cent of its high schools under the new system. Apparently one reason for the slow progress in the NCA was the considerable autonomy of its State Committees, for some NCA states did much better than others.[3] Progress was rapid in the next decade, however. On the occasion of the Association's sixtieth anniversary (1955) the general use of *Evaluative Criteria* and the annual meetings of the state chairmen were hailed as the "most significant advances" of the Commission on Secondary Schools.[4]

When revised *Policies and Criteria* were adopted in 1948, having been overwhelmingly approved by a referendum of the member secondary schools,[5] arrangements were made for a continuing study of the NCA criteria, five to be examined each year.

2. Revision actually began in 1948 with financial support from the General Education Board and from the regional accrediting associations. *NCAQ*, XXXV (January 1951), p. 259. The Cooperative Study is now known as the National Study of School Evaluation.

3. Joseph Roemer, "Progress Report on the Cooperative Study of Secondary School Standards," *The Southern Association Quarterly*, IX (February 1947), pp. 140-143.

4. Milo Bail, "Six Decades of Progress," *NCAQ*, XXX (October 1955), p. 205.

5. Fifty-eight percent of the schools in the Association had replied.

The Commission meanwhile encouraged State Committees to advise a school, which had been warned for violation of a requirement, that it must submit to an evaluation, using the *Evaluative Criteria.*

The new NCA statement on accrediting was divided into Guiding Principles (suggestions that would be helpful for evaluating schools); Policies (specific conditions governing accreditation, e.g.; conditions under which a school might be "warned" or dropped from membership); Regulations (the minimum required for accreditation); and Criteria (the standards of excellence which good schools could use as guidelines for further self-improvement). Procedures suggested by the Cooperative Study were to be followed: first a self-evaluation using check-lists in the *Evaluative Criteria,* then a statement of the school's guiding principles, and finally a visit by an examining team. The effective differences between the old and new approaches lay in the first and second steps. Self-evaluation was a significant innovation and was intended to be the instrument of continuing self-improvement.[6]

"Guiding Principles," as suggested by the Cooperative Study, referred not only to those established by accrediting bodies but to an institution's own purposes and expectations of itself; in short, standards for high schools like those for colleges were to be more flexible and more self-defined than formerly.[7] Moreover, the self-evaluation was based on the participation of teachers—they had not really had much to do under the old system except to see to their own qualifications. One high school principal put it as the Commission's saying to administrators:

> Not only are you permitted—you are now [1950] challenged to call in your staff, your patrons, and . . . your principals and find out what you really want to do. . . . We have to . . . develop, democratically, a philosophy adapted to our

6. Carl A. Jessen, "Cooperative Study of Secondary School Standards after Twenty-One Years," *NCAQ,* XXX (October 1955), pp. 219-225.

7. H. C. Mardis, "What the New Program of Accrediting Secondary Schools Means to Member Schools," *NCAQ,* XXIV (January 1950), pp. 276-283; J. G. Umstattd, "Implications for Use of the 1950 Criteria by State Departments of Education and Local Schools," *National Association of Secondary-School Principals Bulletin,* XXXV (March 1951), pp. 230-240.

local needs and to provide a sound general education program based on the studied needs of our youth. . . . [and] augmented by . . . specialized vocational training. . . ."[8]

It has a contemporary sound at this writing (1969), when some large city "ghetto" schools are being put under direct neighborhood control, and when students are demanding a voice in determining what they should be taught.

Aside from the difficulty of persuading administrators, faculty, and patrons to state and implement their ideals, there is always the question of how much liberty is proper for any public educational institution, i.e., how much it should be permitted to go its own way, and how much it should be required to meet the larger responsibilities demanded by state and nation. This question was partly answered by the growing use of various nationally-rated external tests for college entrance, although these were subject to the criticism of being limited to academic achievement and little else. A problem too in defining a school's objectives, or the "Needs of Youth," as they would be called in the 1950 Cooperative Study *Evaluative Criteria,* was that a school's faculty and administrators seldom seemed able to come down to earth, but instead set goals in high-flown terms that restated the Seven Cardinal Principles. It was often painfully evident that many schools were unable to formulate a realistic philosophy of their own.[9]

Another more immediate problem in enlarging the popular base of evaluation was that the big evaluation teams, locally recruited, tended to "go easy" on each other, particularly if their own schools' evaluations were imminent. And the assessment of a school's operation by "absolute" values in some categories, and by "relative" values in others often required a skill and subtlety that examiners did not really possess, no matter how well-intentioned.[10]

Expanded activity was related also to new issues created by the war and by the changing face of American education. The re-

8. Mardis, p. 278.
9. Jessen, pp. 219-225
10. J. G. Umstattd, "Some Suggestions about the Use of the Evaluative Criteria." *Southern Association Quarterly,* IX (February 1945), pp. 119-123.

turning veteran raised questions about credit for his experiences, for specific training in army schools, or simply for his maturity. The General Educational Development Tests for veterans, which were used by many schools to establish credit, raised the problem of whether such tests merely led to a nationwide external testing program. The use of College Entrance Examination Board tests by an increasing number of colleges, particularly the better ones, further demanded some statement of Association policy. One was forthcoming in 1951. When the Ford Foundation proposed to sponsor a program for accelerating high school courses for gifted students to the extent that some might be ready for college as much as two years ahead of the normal pace, the Commission issued a vigorous dissent.

Only four years later, however, it tentatively approved advanced college standing for courses taken in high school, and the Research and Service Commission established its innovative and highly influential Superior and Talented Students Project. Advanced placement programs developed rapidly from this point, though more slowly in NCA territory than in the Eastern States, and provided, along with the continuing and troublesome athletic issue, a possible base from which to develop improved articulation of high school and college programs.

Other developments raising accreditation questions that were directly related to the return of the veterans were a rash of high school summer schools and correspondence programs offered by proprietary schools hoping to profit from the GI Bill. The main problem with the summer schools was to establish equivalencies in class-time with the regular school term. At first it was expected that the summer schools would be only temporary measures to accommodate veterans, but a variety of circumstances caused them to continue. The solution for accrediting correspondence work was to require that the institution offering such work be under the supervision of the same state department of education as the high school being petitioned to accept credit. Such organizations as the International Correspondence Schools were thereby excluded. High school students taking courses from these schools, especially those taken concurrently with their regular studies, were permitted to do so only under the close supervision of local high schools.

Another postwar development which required the attention of the Association was the continuing educational work of the armed services, in particular the USAFI program and the dependents' schools abroad, both of them the products of a large peacetime military establishment and long-term commitments overseas during the Cold War. The USAFI program of correspondence courses, begun in 1941 and assumed at the start to be a temporary accommodation for young men whose education had been interrrupted, became even larger after the war. Operated from Madison, Wisconsin, the program had excellent academic —as well as patriotic—credentials, and in time its work was not only acceptable for high school credit, but a special subcommittee of the Secondary Commission authorized a high school unit of study to inform high school students of the educational opportunities offered in the services.[11]

None of the new situations afforded as unique a venture for the Association as the accreditation of schools for dependents of American servicemen stationed abroad. The Dependents' Schools Service was organized in May 1946 in the European command, and the first schools opened the following October. Thirty-eight elementary schools and five high schools, all in Germany, enrolled 2,800 children. By 1955-1956 the program had expanded to include schools in Asia and Puerto Rico as well as in all of Europe, and enrolled in excess of 60,000 children.

The first high schools, the five in Germany, were accredited by the NCA in 1947. During the first year of operation, the Army Schools' Director of Education, Virgil R. Walker, had written to the NCA Commission on Secondary Schools inquiring about the possibility of North Central accreditation of the five high schools. Walker was asked to provide more information and to arrange for a visit to the schools and a report to the Association by Virgil

11. See Charles W. Boardman, "The Educational Program of the United States Armed Forces Institute," *NCAQ*, XXX (October 1955), pp. 333-343.

Rogers, the Battle Creek, Michigan schools superintendent, who was on an assignment in Europe for the Department of the Army.

The NCA had taken a momentous step; heretofore it had steadfastly refused to accredit any school outside its area.[12] But there remained serious questions, which had not really been settled, about such matters as the suitability of buildings and school supplies, the adequacy and continuity of the teaching force (teachers were being recruited on short leaves, usually two years, from their home positions), the small size and isolation of the widely scattered schools, and especially the possible interferences by the services through the officer who was technically responsible for the schools.

Another question that has never really been properly faced, was the propriety of contributing to the cultural isolation of the American community abroad. Considerable adverse comment about the insulation of servicemen's families would appear in time, usually with reference to the huge commissaries, bowling alleys, and the segregated housing provided by the U. S. Government. But among the tightest little islands of all were the dependents' schools. These could have profited hugely, it would seem, if the NCA's evaluative criteria had been used to create an individual philosophy and special character.

In any event, the NCA had accepted the unaccustomed responsibility, and it even partly institutionalized its procedures that first year by appointing a committee to supervise the dependents' schools. This committee took the role of a State Committee, duly processing reports and referring them to the reviewing committees in the usual way. An important hurdle was cleared in the early 1950's when the NCA won its contention that full and unhampered direction of the educational programs abroad must be in the hands of professional civilian educators. The appointment of experienced school superintendents to direct the several area

12. For example, in 1943 the NCA refused to accredit the American Institute in La Paz, Bolivia, on the ground that it accredited no schools outside the continental limits of the United States.

programs on a relatively long-term basis completed the incorporation of the dependents' schools into the world of American high schools.

The other regional associations were notified of the NCA's new venture soon after it began, and in 1950 a conference of representatives from the associations and from the overseas education divisions of the services agreed that, since the NCA had gone further in developing an accreditation procedure, it should be designated the official accrediting body for all of the associations. The conference also agreed "that it was desirable to set up . . . direct contact with the schools by representatives of the Association . . . that funds be provided [by military services] to finance a visiting team of two or three representatives so that normal procedures be approximated." Representatives of the Armed Services were present at the conference and concurred in the recommendations.[13]

Beneath the exciting challenges and novel experiences of this revolutionary era there still remained the day-to-day routine of seeing that high schools and colleges in nineteen states not only maintained an acceptable educational performance but strove constantly to improve themselves. Whatever new vistas the future might promise, the facts of the situation were that a great many high schools of mid-America were near the bare minimum of acceptability.

For example, as previously noted, one of their most glaring weaknesses was the inadequacy of their libraries. In 1956, of the librarians employed in approved schools, over 1,400 had fewer than six semester credits of training in library management, the minimum recommended by the Cooperative Study. What to do about libraries had already been the subject of a number of inconclusive discussions when the library study commissioned by the Research and Service Commission in 1954 was approved as a

13. Edgar G. Johnston, "A Decade of Dependents' Schools," *NCAQ*, XXXII (January 1958), pp. 240-255. It should be noted that other accrediting associations, particularly the Middle States and the Southern, assumed similar responsibilities for other types of American schools abroad, among them private institutions and those maintained and operated under the United States Department of State.

long-range goal. Even then a number of practical considerations prevented any immediate improvement. The recommendations on training for librarians excited apprehensions in the schools because librarians were in short supply. Some practical questions also arose about the discrepancy between the relatively high requirements for librarians and the modest recommendations on library holdings. How much professional training was really needed to manage a book collection that was increased by fewer than one hundred books annually? Chairmen of several state committees were quick to point out that many otherwise accredited schools might lose their standing without a real chance to meet the newly established requirement if the implementation of the report were not delayed—which indeed it was when it became clear that immediate compliance was actually impossible.

One immediate result of the new regulations was a sudden burst of prosperity for library schools, particularly in those colleges and universities chiefly responsible for supplying the needs of their state school system. Meanwhile, a beginning had been made toward a basic improvement too long neglected for other things considerably less important than books. One of the marked changes in secondary schools in the next dozen years was the improvement in the quality and the use of their libraries, and the changed outlook this represented.

Academic improvement was also the object of the Secondary Commission's efforts to control the ever-widening variety of contests that had developed in and around the secondary schools. Although one could hardly call contests and their control a central educational issue, they were the kind of problem that had a way of intruding into more important discussions, just as they also intruded into the more central concerns of the schools.

In part, non-athletic competitions were a holdover from the day of the long defunct literary society activities of the colleges; in part they had been encouraged as an antidote to the concentration on athletics, a compensatory opportunity to recognize the non-athletes. They were also a part of the inter-community rivalries among small towns where the high school was the center of activity and entertainment, or in the cities where they could become linked to racial or class tensions. Such forces, organized by local boosters or by larger groups outside the immediate area of the school, could exert irresistible pressures upon a school. Whatever the circumstances or original rationale, the relation of contests and winning to education was a matter of rising concern by the end of the 1930's.

When the war began more than seventy-five organizations were in the business of encouraging or sponsoring school contests. By 1946 the number was reduced by half, with about a dozen approved by the Secondary Commission. This was a stopgap measure rather than a solution, and in 1946 the Secondary Commission established a Contest Committee to devise criteria for the judgment of contest-sponsoring organizations. Five years later the committee presented its first report to the Commission with recommendations for the regulation of contests in music and speech. The recommendations were actually an endorsement of the position of the Music Educators' National Conference and the Speech Association of America, which the NCA committee had agreed to support following conferences with representatives of the two professional organizations. Detailed suggestions were offered for curricula in the two subjects, with public performances approved only as part of the intrinsic training in the subject; the committee emphatically disapproved the emphasis on winning.[14]

Some strong support for the NCA effort was generated from the associations of the teachers of the subjects involved, as well as from the National Association of Secondary School Principals. Yet by the mid-1950's control of contests was still unsatisfactory. A new committee, replacing the old Contests Committee, was formed to make the usual survey of the situation in the states of the Association. State chairmen were also talking about it, and

14. Lowell Fisher, "Further Activities of the Contest Committee of the Commission on Secondary Schools," NCAQ, XXVI (October 1951), pp. 202-226.

indeed made it the chief topic of their ninth annual meeting in 1955.

Eventually the new committee presented a report which was largely the work of a group composed of the chairmen of the NCA Activities Committee and of the Contests and Activities Committee of the National Association of Secondary School Principals, and four representatives of the executive committee of the Music Educators National Conference. This statement was approved by the Commission on Secondary Schools in 1957.[15] It was intended to be the first of a series of such jointly formulated statements about every school subject affected by interscholastic contests. The root of the problem was that the schools served several masters, not the least important of which were the local communities, and that whatever administrators, professional societies, teachers, and accrediting associations might say to the contrary, the communities—and the promoters—remained unconvinced that contests were undesirable.

Although frustrated—or at least delayed—in its efforts to stop excessive competition by the local autonomy that is a feature of American education, the Secondary Commission would score several impressive victories over local autonomy in the years after the war. These victories would have all the significance for the NCA in its claims to the right to accredit that the Langer case[16] of 1938 had for the Higher Commission. The issues of the Langer case and the school cases (they did not really get to court) were practically identical, i.e., the measure of independence an educational institution, or to be more exact, an administration, is to have from a board of directors or public officials in matters that are considered professional. On these issues the Secondary Commission faced the stiffest kind of challenge, and won. As George Rosenlof, secretary of the Secondary Commission put it: "We faced these matters valiantly and courageously. We stood our ground."

The issues underlying the two major contests of the Associa-

15. "Report of the Activities Committee of the Commission on Secondary Schools of the North Central Association, 1956-57," NCAQ, XXXII (January 1958), pp. 256-263.
16. See p. 57n.

tion versus boards, those of Chicago and Kansas City, were "improper" interference in school affairs by the one and the failure to provide adequate financing of its schools by the other. The Chicago case, which had been under investigation for a considerable time, came up for decision in 1947, and the Secondary Commission voted to drop all high schools in the second largest city in the country from its accredited list until political appointees were eliminated from the school board and the Otis Law (which divided the authority of the school administration into a triumvirate, each member of which was responsible only to the Board of Education) was repealed. There were also charges that the politically appointed board members were interfering improperly in the operation of the superintendent's office.

The Commission's action may have been a little overplayed because at the time that the Association acted, an amendment to the objectionable Otis Law was already before the Illinois legislature, and the Chicago mayor had already set in motion a non-partisan procedure for nominating members to the school board. However, the NCA could claim with some justification that these actions would not have been secured without previous threats of disaccreditation. In any event, shortly following the Commission's action in March, the NCA conditions had been substantially met.

In the Kansas City case of 1950 the issue was less the presumed or potential malfeasance in school governance than it was the failure of a board—and its Constituency—to finance its schools adequately. Ordinarily such matters were difficult to handle, since the schools of any major city in 1950 were probably far above the minimum level for accreditation, but the NCA's case was based on the Kansas City board's decision to reduce the length of the school term because of a shortage of funds. In effect, the NCA seized a technical violation to compel a community to tax itself more heavily for school support than it had previously been willing to do. Again the board of a major city complied rather than face the loss of NCA membership and the disapproval of its constituency that would inevitably result.

Disciplining Jefferson County, Colorado, and Hamtramck,

Michigan, were other relatively impressive instances of the NCA's using disaccreditation or the threat of it to force school boards to follow certain procedures. In the first instance, which occurred in 1954, a school board established the office of superintendent of construction and comptroller independent of the superintendent's office. The situation was corrected before final action was taken against the school district.

In Hamtramck, the problem was the dismissal of a superintendent without a hearing. The board, called to account by the Michigan State Committee, refused its demand that the dismissal be rescinded and the superintendent be given a hearing. Hamtramck was accordingly put on "warning." The action aroused considerable angry press comment about intervention in a local school by an "outside" agency, a not uncommon reaction when the Association acted against a board or a school system to enforce certain procedures protecting the rights of personnel.

Boards and the public still tended to look upon accreditation as approval of their having met certain quantitative requirements such as adequate equipment, or teachers having a requisite number of credits to teach certain courses. Local communities resented intervention in such self-government prerogatives as the employment or dismissal of teachers, and it is doubtful if many really understood, if they even knew about, Criterion 4B(3) of the *Policies, Regulations, and Criteria* as amended in 1950 to the effect that "Employees who are to be dismissed or refused re-employment [must be] given reasons for the action taken by the board of education and . . . given an opportunity for a hearing before official action is taken." As a matter of fact, the Secondary Commission's application of the criterion was limited almost entirely to boards' relations with superintendents.

On some issues the Association's influence appears to have been small, or not even applied. Teaching salaries remained relatively low, averaging from $2,400 to $2,600 for men and about $600 less for women in 1946. To be sure, some State Committees did exert pressure from time to time to improve salaries, and on occasion a school was dropped from the accredited list because of the inability or the unwillingness of a community to finance an adequate level of education. (Note the instance of Kansas City.) On the whole, however, there is little evidence in the records that the NCA did much that was truly effective in the matter of salaries, or in narrowing the rather large differential between teaching and administrative salaries. Some publicized guidelines to put teachers' salaries on a competitive basis with the compensation for other professions or administration might have been as effective a measure as any to improve secondary education. Moreover, such recommendations would seem to have been no less in order than rules on library expenditures or on teachers' training. As it was, the quality of secondary school personnel undoubtedly suffered because of poor financial rewards for good teaching, even in the schools themselves.

Nor did the Secondary Commission appear to offer more than private expressions of concern about the effects of McCarthyism and witch-hunting in general upon the quality of high school education. Yet the high schools, being closer to their constituencies and more directly subject to their governing boards than most colleges, undoubtedly suffered more, if less spectacularly, from efforts to control opinions than the colleges did.

It must be said in defense of the Association, however, that the decade of the 1950's was not the most opportune time to embark upon a vigorous expansion of Association activities into areas as sensitive as salaries and public expression. Accreditation by "outside" bodies was already coming under some criticism. In one state, Illinois, criticism of "interference" by the Secondary Commission got beyond mere grumbling. The Peoria Board of Education, following what its members took to be high-handed treatment by a representative of the NCA in 1949, prevailed upon the Illinois School Board Association to appoint a committee to investigate the relationship between the school boards of Illinois and accrediting agencies, especially the NCA.

Fortunately, a move that originated in a spirit of pique became an earnest effort to develop a workable relationship between the Association and local authority. The school board investigators argued with considerable effect that since the State Committees were presumably representative, they should have school board members on them, and they recommended that the Illinois State Committee be altered to include seven professional members and seven school board members. The committee in turn approved the idea and recommended to the Secondary Commission that a half-professional, half-lay (school board members) state committee be organized accordingly on an experimental basis, beginning in 1952.[17]

Meantime, the Illinois State Legislature had passed a bill (1951) authorizing "an investigation of the North Central Association." Actions of this sort, plus the obvious misunderstanding all too often of what the NCA really was and did caused considerable concern. Milo Bail, president of the Association in 1952, proposed a series of conferences in the NCA states to acquaint the public with the Association's function.[18] From here it was only a short distance to the inevitable committee, this one created in 1953 with instructions to formulate an effective public information program.

17. Lowell B. Fisher, "The Illinois School Board Association and the North Central Association," *NCAQ*, XXV (January 1951), pp. 280-284; W. C. Jacquin, "Boards of Education and the North Central Association," *NCAQ*, XXVI (January 1952), pp. 248-251.
18. *NCAQ*, XXVII (October 1952), pp. 248-250.

III

An Expanding View

Transition to a concept of relating institutional quality to the encouragement of individuality in institutions—"doing one's thing," as today's hippies say—was not without its problems, a good many of which were yet unanswered in the middle 1950's. The main one, in particular with relation to new community colleges and technical-vocational schools, which were appearing in increasing numbers, arose out of the Commission on Colleges and Universities' insistence that any curricular structure must be built around a core of general education if it were to qualify for accredited collegiate status. Many new institutions found this, however loosely defined, too restrictive for their purposes and not infrequently went their own way without bothering with NCA recognition. Could or should the NCA accept their limited definitions of education as properly individualistic, or should it stick to its older ideal at the possible cost of compromising its own declared policy? The Commission on Secondary Schools found it perhaps even more difficult to translate individuality into working policy because the high schools were being pressured by their constituencies to move in the direction of tradition rather than innovation. Innovation in the schools had to be handled with great circumspection in the public climate of the 1950's.

It would be an error to infer, however, that the problems of pushing forward a new policy meant any weakening of the principle of general accreditation by educational institutions' own organizations. Indeed, in the case of the NCA, particularly in the area of higher education, the principle had become more firmly established than ever, and several possible threats to regional self-accreditation had been turned aside. A growing movement toward accreditation by disciplines, rather than by institutions, had been headed off, for the time at least, by vigorous action from the institutions.

The National Commission on Accrediting, formed in 1949 to combat the movement, managed to limit the number of disciplinary accrediting bodies and supported the regional associations' effort to incorporate their activities into general accreditation practices.[1] A possibility that some of the more ardent enthusiasts in the National Commission might establish their own general body to replace the regional associations came to nothing. Meantime, the last national body of any prestige to continue a semblance of general accreditation, the Association of American Universities, abandoned all of its institution-rating activities in 1949.

Concrete endorsement of the regional associations' position came from both private and public agencies. When the Ford Foundation made a half billion dollars available for grants to colleges and universities in the mid-1950's, the first stipulation was that applicants must be accredited.[2] Other philanthropic organizations tended to observe the same limitation. Such endorsements were soon to be augmented immeasurably after Federal funds became available for educational institutions, because the United States Office of Education adopted the policy of relying on the evaluations of the regional associations as a basis for determining institutional eligibility for grants.

In addition, the regional associations had behind them the

1. Accreditation was the subject of numerous articles in education journals during the late 1940's and 1950's. For a general account of the accreditation movement and various approaches to it see William K. Selden, *Accreditation: A Struggle over Standards in Higher Education* (New York: Harper and Brothers, 1960).

2. Manning Pattillo, "The Meaning of Accreditation," (duplicated typescript, March 1956).

weight of a Federal Court ruling in 1938 when Governor William Langer of North Dakota had failed in an effort to reverse the disaccreditation of the North Dakota Agricultural College by taking the matter to court. Both the U. S. District Court and the U. S. Circuit Court of Appeals found for the NCA. (The Association's ground for removing the college from its accredited list was that the governor was interfering directly in administrative and faculty appointments.)[3]

The Commission on Secondary Schools was on less certain ground because state departments of education were preempting many of its functions and because accreditation of a high school was decreasing in importance for college entrance. Yet it was clearly in no danger of extinction in the 1950's. Its accrediting still meant much to a school and to its community, more than ever before it seemed; even Chicago, Kansas City, and Jefferson County, Colorado had proved unwilling to face the consequences of disaccreditation, however unspecific those consequences might be in practice. Moreover, the Secondary Commission was moving to strengthen its position in local communities by taking pains to meet its public and explain itself, and by broadening the participation in the accrediting process.

Of more fundamental concern was the course that education would take. During the late 1940's and early 1950's American education, especially in the high schools, came in for much criticism, usually to the effect that courses lacked substance and that the schools were overly permissive and lenient. The launching of the first space vehicle by the Russians in 1957 focused criticism on the schools which were charged with the responsibility for losing the Cold War. For the accrediting associations the situation raised the question of how to stiffen the curriculum while heading off trends toward elitism for those few who could excel in mathematics and the sciences.

3. Davis, p. 35; for a full account of the case, "The State of North Dakota, by William Langer, Governor, Plaintiff, vs. North Central Association of Colleges and Secondary Schools, a Voluntary Association, et al., Defendants," NCAQ, XIII (April 1939), pp. 505-517.

The civil rights issue, dramatized and given force by the Brown vs. Topeka decision of 1954 outlawing school segregation, reinforced the ideal of inclusiveness in the face of elitism. It also posed a moral problem for the Association. Could the NCA any longer follow the course of accepting society as it was, as it had generally done before 1954, or must it not use its power to uphold the constitutional and legal rights of the Negro?

On the more immediate operational level, there was the prospect of greatly expanded Federal assistance to education. Such aid had steadily grown since the war through the GI bills, and through loans or grants for research and for capital construction. In 1958 the National Defense Education Act began a program of direct assistance to college students. Until the middle 1950's the new assistance went mostly to the colleges, but the prospects of broader aid were imminent under the Elementary and Secondary Education Act of 1965. The problems reared were numerous, the most ominous for the Association being the possibility of national accreditation, and for the schools it was the possibility that Federal needs—or Congressional idiosyncrasies—would determine the directions taken by the schools and universities.

And there remained also the new institutions—the vocational-technical schools and the community colleges—all of which existed to serve a community, or human or occupational needs. Yet such schools obviously failed to qualify by conventional standards for Association membership. As late as 1956 the NCA still insisted that it would not extend its accreditation to institutions that did not offer "a substantial program" in general or liberal education.

Another aspect of the changing shape of American higher education was the emerging importance of the urban-oriented university. Increasingly, from the mid-1950's American higher education was reflecting the urbanization of American society. State universities, most of them situated in semi-isolated small towns, were beginning to respond to demands from the cities to establish urban branches, and the old half-ignored and half-financed municipal universities found themselves beginning to enjoy an unaccustomed public favor—which in due time would lead them from mainly relying on municipal support to state financing.[4]

Other problems, some of them not even foreseen in the early 1950's, were also to arise in the not too distant future. One of the most fundamental questions concerned the base of representation in the NCA. The Illinois school boards challenged their exclusion from the State Committee in 1952, and it was not too long before the American Association of University Professors came forward with a statement on the role of faculty in accrediting. Including high school teachers and college professors on examination teams as was already being done, or occasionally putting a school board member on State Committees, as was done in Colorado and a few other states, were not really answers to concerns about the almost undiluted control of the Commissions and the Executive Committee of the Association by high school and college administrators and professors from a single discipline—Education. The rise of faculty power, which had quietly but steadily advanced in the colleges for more than a generation, was a trend which accrediting agencies would have to consider.

Prospects for the future indicated an expansion of Association activities at a rate no less than that of the decade since the war: annual membership dues for high schools had risen from $5.00 to $15.00 between 1945 and 1955; in the same period the budget had climbed from $7,650 to $24,079 for the Secondary Commission, and from $6,022 to $35,935 for the Higher Commission. Total expenditures of the Association quadrupled between 1942 and 1954, from $33,000 to $115,000. (They tripled again in the next decade.) By the mid-1950's the work load of operating the NCA was clearly getting beyond the capacities of the unpaid volunteers upon whom the Association had depended since its founding. The secretaryship and the position of *Quarterly* editor,

4. For some comments on the urban universities' importance see Norman Burns, "Changing Concepts of Higher Education," *NCAQ*, XXXVIII (Spring 1964), pp. 296-300.

in particular, were heavy responsibilities, too much to expect of professors who also had to keep up the duties of full-time university appointments.

The process of adjustment was already under way in the early 1950's. A new Committee on Reorganization of the Association (previously known as the Committee on Evaluation of the Association and as the Implementation Committee) appointed in 1952, recommended revisions in the constitution and Association procedures in late 1953, including the employment of a paid secretary for the Association.

In 1954, Norman Burns, secretary of the Higher Commission, speaking before the Conference of State Chairmen, presented a plan to reorganize the Commission on Colleges and Universities. It had the four-fold purpose of completing the transition from quantitative to qualitative evaluation, of de-emphasizing inspection and emphasizing service, of developing procedures and criteria to accommodate to the multi-purpose system of higher education that was emerging, and of developing a corps of expert evaluators from within the membership of the Association. Burns contended that his Commission had been spending far too much of its time in nursing along marginal institutions at the expense of supplying innovative leadership for higher education.

An imaginative move, it was a response to the realization that a major educational revolution was in progress, and that a new receptiveness was abroad in the Association.

PART TWO

Promoting Constructive Change 1955-1970

IV

The Association and a New Era

In effect, the spirit of innovation would involve moving beyond the traditional assumptions of what the schools and colleges were supposed to be. As never before, the Association and its constituency were of the world, buffeted and swayed by social and economic tensions and by the ever-changing demands of a dynamic society. The Association could elect to take the precarious and uncharted road of social engineering, or the more traditional—and safer—one of adapting the schools to whatever changes emerged. In either case, it was essential that the Association's leaders assess their situation, establish priorities, and devise new services. It had to be guide and leader, the articulate spokesman for a relevant educational ideal, and the source of information and advice gathered from its collective experience and tested by its own research. Whatever the degree of relative immunity certain schools and colleges might enjoy from serious interference by the Association, they, as well as the less prestigious, were in serious need of all the help and advice they could get. It was a rare institution in the late 1950's that did not find its problems multiplying faster than its resources to meet them.

These problems were highlighted by the dramatic intervention of Federal financial assistance for education. The sheer magnitude of the Federal Government's contributions after the 1950's, plus general acceptance of education's central role in defense, economic development, and social adjustment, placed the educational establishment in a flattering role, and also made it vulnerable to becoming a weathervane for every national emergency or a tool for the public policies of the moment.

The full possibilities of Federal assistance were first brought home to educators and the public when the Report of the President's Commission on Higher Education revealed in 1947 that $1,772,000,000 in Federal funds had been expended on higher education during the fiscal year ending June 30, 1947. To be sure, all but $100,000,000 could be explained as "temporary" spending for veterans' readjustment. A more important point in the report was the recommendation that colleges and universities prepare to increase their enrollments to 4,600,000 by 1960, a staggering number which would only be accommodated if new sources of funds were tapped. A bill to establish a Federal scholarship program, to a maximum of $150,000,000 per year by 1952, was introduced into the Eighty-First Congress.[1] The long-range effects of such headlong expansion could only be surmised at the time, although overcrowding of facilities and shortages of faculty and equipment were a practical certainty, with a decline of educational quality a strong possibility.

Although the scholarship program was not approved, by 1963 enrollments were rising even faster than the predicted rate, and other kinds of Federal assistance had passed $4,000,000,000 per year. (This sum would be more than doubled by 1968, and was expected to climb to $20,000,000,000 by 1975.) A "landmark in the evolution of Federal relations to education" was the passage of the National Defense Education Act of 1958 authorizing appropriations of something over a billion dollars over a four-year period beginning in 1959.[2]

1. James E. Russell, *Federal Activities in Higher Education After The Second World War* (New York: Columbia University, King's Crown Press, 1951), pp. 2, 12. See also Hollis P. Allen, *The Federal Government and Education: The Original and Complete Study for the Hoover Commission Task Force on Public Welfare* (New York: McGraw-Hill, 1950).
2. "The Federal Government and Higher Education," *Higher Education in the United States,* American Council on Education (Washington, D.C., 1961), pp. 58-67.

In fiscal 1962, the Department of Defense alone had a $520,000,000 "involvement" in education and a score of other Federal agencies were supporting their own schools, providing scholarships and research grants, or otherwise using educational facilities. The Agency for International Development, for example, was spending $100,000,000 annually on educational assistance abroad; seventy colleges and universities held AID contracts in 1962. The Peace Corps had contracts in 1963 with forty-two colleges for on-campus training in the amount of $5,600,000, and the National Institutes of Health spent about $35,000,000 to support 10,000 graduate students in medical and related scientific training. Other agencies with similar multi-million dollar programs in education included the National Science Foundation, the Public Health Service, the Atomic Energy Commission, the National Aeronautics and Space Administration, and the Office of Vocational Rehabilitation.[3]

And the end was nowhere in sight. In 1968, when colleges and university enrollments were near the 7,000,000 mark, about 10 percent of them graduate students (there were about 300,000 in 1960), forty-two university presidents issued an appeal to the United States Government to provide financial aid for operating expenses on every level, from junior college to graduate and professional school. Scholarships, buildings, research grants were no longer enough.[4]

By this time, the colleges were not alone in being directly affected by Federal programs. Such measures as the Manpower Development and Training Act of 1962, the Vocational Education Act of 1963, and the Economic Opportunity Act of 1964 (the anti-poverty bill) vitally affected the elementary and high schools, since the bills drew attention to the fact that their vocational courses were outdated and unrealistic. Remedial reading, guidance counseling, study centers, Saturday classes, summer

3. Harry Kursh, *The United States Office of Education: A Century of Service* (Philadelphia: Chilton Books, 1963).
4. *New York Times,* Sunday Education Section, June 30, 1968.

schools, and the like were all either introduced or emphasized by the Federal programs.[5]

Although from time to time various NCA spokesmen commented on the implications of the developments, and Association representatives on occasion met with such bodies as the American Council on Education to discuss the implications of governmental policies, the Association had had only a minor role in originating or determining the direction of such assistance or anticipating its effects. However, it was placed in a strategic position to influence policy when it was invited to act as an evaluating and reviewing agency for the Government. One of the fortunate aspects of the situation, as far as the preservation of the Association's independent position was concerned, was that the United States Office of Education, having been neglected for years, was ill-equipped to initiate an accreditation program of its own. The regional associations with their well-established procedures and their long experience were convenient nonpolitical agencies for passing judgment on the worthiness of institutions applying for Federal funds.

Following the passage of the Higher Education Facilities Act in 1963, the Office of Education turned directly to the regional associations for help in evaluating applications. Tentative procedures hastily established in 1964 were gradually formalized, again on request from the Office of Education, for other Federal programs.

Bringing the Association into line with the new trends would be no mere matter of an executive decision. Leadership and conciliation were required in a body that had a good deal of "establishment" about it, and that had some long-standing differences between the two groups represented: the high schools and the colleges. Changes within the commissions could be managed fairly well, for they had achieved something of a consensus on goals and procedures. On the Association level, however, the two accrediting commissions were not always in agreement on policy.

5. Gordon Cawelti, "Poverty and the Schools," *NCAQ*, XXXIX (Winter 1965), pp. 242-244.

It will be recalled that in the effort to reform interscholastic and intercollegiate athletics, the high schools and the smaller colleges had been overpowered by the large universities which refused to accept a policy that probably a majority of the schools and colleges seemed to want.

For the most part, the Secondary Commission was the one that regularly promoted the case for articulating secondary and collegiate education. Numerous demands for "reform" directed to the Commission on Colleges and Universities, by implication at least, included expressions of concern about the lack of continuity between high school and college curricula, insufficient cooperation on admissions and athletic policies, and the growing practice among the colleges of using external tests in preference to high school records as the basis for admissions. Articulation was never given the attention by the colleges that the high school spokesmen thought it deserved.[6] A major concern was that the enormous expansion of college attendance was in danger of turning high school programs increasingly toward college preparation while programs that served the students unlikely to attend college were neglected.

The Secondary Commission's Committee on School and College Relations presented a lengthy although somewhat inconclusive report in 1961 suggesting such cooperative measures as inviting college and university representatives to participate in high school accreditation examinations, expanding the interchangeability of high school and college courses along the lines developed by the Advanced Placement Program, and generally using State Committees as intermediaries to improve high school-college relations. As a first step the committee urged that meetings of high school and college representatives be held in each of the nineteen NCA states. In 1963 the committee was merged into a comparable committee of the Research and Service Commission.

A Long-Range Planning Committee report in 1963 on the goals, functions, and procedures of the Association identified the

6. Stephen Romine, "The North Central Association—A Look to the Future," *NCAQ*, XXXV (October 1960), p. 179.

central problem as the failure to coordinate the relationships of the three commissions with each other or to coordinate their relationships with the Association generally—in short, to the failure of articulation in the NCA's own central councils. A major difficulty was that the two accrediting commissions employed "quite different measures for evaluating educational institutions. . . ." Identifying the problem and solving it were two different matters, in part because of "a lack of coordination and communication between the Secondary and Higher Commissions on the state level." Also at issue was a question of the proper division of power between the higher and secondary branches of the NCA. This was the main point in the formal complaint to the Association Executive Committee filed by the secondary state chairmen in 1956, and of questions raised a decade later in a special report presented over the name of the chairman of the Secondary Commission.[7]

Actually, the complaints were not as barren of result as their persistent recurrence might indicate. Centralizing the Association offices and developing a paid secretariat were solid steps toward an improved coordination of activities. Illustrative of the problem was the fact that until 1960 NCA offices were scattered over the territory, wherever the current incumbents happened to be employed. The secretary of the Association, Charles W. Boardman, was professor emeritus at the University of Minnesota, and therefore the Association secretarial office was likewise in Minneapolis. The Secondary Commission secretary, Alva Gibson, kept his office in Charleston, West Virginia. The secretary of the Commission on Colleges and Universities, Norman Burns, had his offices on the campus of the University of Chicago. And the editor of the *Quarterly* and head of Association publications, Harlan Koch, was located at the University of Michigan where he was an administrator.

In 1954, the NCA constitution was amended to permit the

7. "Report of the Special Committee on the Memorandum from the State Chairmen (approved by the Commission on Secondary Schools)," October 14-16, 1956; Richard C. Krebs, "Special Report to the Board of Directors, NCA," Spring 1966.

payment of salaries to the general secretary of the Association and to the secretary of the Commission on Colleges and Universities.[8] A Long-Range Planning Committee, appointed in 1957 to consider the problem, recommended that several offices be consolidated and relocated in one place. In 1960 Norman Burns accepted the additional duties of secretary of the Association, editor of the *Quarterly,* and head of public relations—he continued in his old office of secretary of the Higher Commission. Anne Stameshkin, assistant to Secretary Boardman, was appointed associate secretary of the Association and associate editor of the *Quarterly.* Two years later when Gordon Cawelti, assistant director of the Laboratory School at the University of Iowa, was appointed secretary of the Secondary Commission, his offices were also moved to Chicago.

Headquarters were temporarily located in the offices of the Commission on Colleges and Universities on the University of Chicago campus pending final decision to buy, construct, or rent suitable offices. In 1961, the offices were moved to another "temporary" location in a suite of rooms at the Shoreland Hotel, a few blocks off the university campus. Eight years later the Association was still housed in the Shoreland, partly because relationships of the commissions to the Association had not yet been fully defined. In 1963, for example, the Secondary Commission was unwilling to approve a Long-Range Planning Committee recommendation to move ahead with plans for acquiring a headquarters until the administrative arrangements of the Association had been altered to its satisfaction. A few members of the Secondary Commission went so far as to suggest the wisdom of moving back to a separate headquarters or even seceding entirely from the Association. Undoubtedly these were often merely expressions of individual disgruntlement, but they could not help but dampen enthusiasm for an expensive move. A more compelling consideration was that, shabby though the once grand old Shoreland had become, its advantages—low rent and convenience—

8. "Gratuitous Services No Longer Adequate for the Work of the Association," *NCAQ,* XXIX (October 1954), p. 149.

outweighed many of the prospective advantages of an expensive new building.

Indeed, centralization had raised another issue, which remained unresolved at the end of the 1960's. This arose from the decision to combine the offices of secretary of the Association with secretary of the Commission on Colleges and Universities. When the Planning Committee attempted finally to solve the dilemma by combining the office of secretary of the Commission on Research and Service (to be elevated to a salaried full-time position) with the office of secretary of the Association, the Commission on Colleges and Universities rejected it.

In 1963 the Long-Range Planning Committee circulated a report attempting to define the points of difference among the commissions. This in turn led to an unprecedented meeting of the governing boards of the Association and the three commissions to consider the proper limitations of NCA activities, means for improved cooperation among the commissions, and projections of whatever additional financial burdens could be anticipated to accompany new developments. One of the more immediate measures to balance conflicting interests was to give each commission equal membership in the Executive Committee of the Association and to change the memberships of the paid secretaries who sat on the committee from voting to nonvoting status.[9]

Beneath what might be viewed superficially as a mere power struggle lay a serious division on general policy, and differences in methods and outlook. Representatives of the secondary schools frequently hinted, if they did not charge outright, that too large a proportion of the Association's energies and income were diverted from the central work of accreditation in favor of visionary schemes that only the college membership or its secretary thought worthwhile. A specific instance of what such critics thought to be an unnecessary diversion of energy and attention was Burns's active role in creating a federation of the regional associations' commissions on higher education. For his part, Burns viewed the federation move as a step toward the independent development of

9. Article VI, Amended NCA Bylaws, 1965.

national uniformity in accreditation practices which was made necessary by the rapid growth of Federal assistance to schools and colleges. (Two years later, however, the secretaries of the secondary commissions of the regional associations were meeting informally to discuss common concerns. In 1969 John A. Stanavage, newly appointed executive secretary of the NCA Secondary Commission, was elected to a two-year term as chairman of the Council on Regional Secondary School Accrediting Commissions.)

The movement toward unifying the higher education branches of the regional associations had been in progress for years. As early as 1949, when criticism of accreditation was at its height, an American Council on Education conference of association representatives had established a National Committee of Regional Accrediting Agencies to which each association was asked to name a representative.[10] One of its purposes was to consider creation of a national federation. More or less regular meetings began with this move. For a considerable period thereafter, however, cooperation remained mostly on an informal basis of exchanging representatives to annual meetings, the sharing of information, and the like. The one major exception was the delegation of accreditation and supervision of Dependents' Schools to the North Central Association.

Sentiment for more than this was revived when in 1962 the college commissions adopted a resolution proposed by Norman Burns that the regional associations cooperate formally in evaluating doctoral programs. A year later, the National Committee, of which Burns was chairman, formally proposed the establishment of a Federation of Regional Accrediting Commissions of Higher Education. The proposal was endorsed by the NCA Commission on Colleges and Universities in 1963, and the Federation was formally organized and held the first of its annual meetings on March 2, 1964.[11] The move had been hastened in large part,

10. *NCAQ*, XXIV (July 1949), p. 11.
11. National Committee of Regional Accrediting Agencies Draft proposal, "That There Be Established the Federation of Accrediting Commissions of

after years of talk and sporadic efforts, by the necessity to establish common norms and procedures to deal with the United States Government.

The Federation council chosen by the member associations was to meet once each year. Its duties included (1) codifying, developing, and specifying the general principles of institutional evaluation to govern general accrediting; (2) promoting interchange of personnel in policy-making bodies and visiting teams; and (3) establishing temporary committees to deal with special problems, such as uniform policies on graduate programs, and uniform working relationships with the Federal Government and the various agencies which granted funds for special programs. Despite some objections from the Secondary Commission, the Association approved the proposal and likewise the selection of Burns as the Federation's first secretary.

Federation was a response to two challenges almost in direct contradiction of each other. On the one hand, there was the urgent necessity for the associations to come to some agreement on a set of policies and standards for schools seeking to qualify for Federal assistance grants before the Federal Government set its own standards and thereby thrust them on the voluntary associations. At the same time Federation played some part in alleviating the threat of disunity created by professional accreditation. Since the formation of the National Commission on Accrediting in 1949, the movement to limit individual professional accrediting of sections of institutions, by departments for example, had been continuous. The National Commission proposed in 1952 that the regional associations work toward eventually assuming responsibility for all accreditation in higher education, "general as well as professional." Although accreditation by professional bodies had not been stopped, it had been brought under some measure of control, at least to the extent of limiting such accreditation to one body for each recognized vocation or profession (there were

Higher Education," March 7, April 18, 1963; Norman Burns (ed.), "Higher Commissions Federate," *NCAQ*, XXXVIII (Spring 1964), p. 273; Articles of Agreement, *Ibid.*, pp. 274-275.

two for Law), and few if any for the specific disciplines or departments.[12]

It would be misleading, however, to assume that the problem of coordinating general and professional accreditation had been fully solved, not even to the extent that it was handled uniformly among the regional associations. The Middle States Association, for example, included professional representatives on its college evaluation teams, which as a consequence could be as many as seventy people.[13] In the NCA area the professional accrediting agencies usually made their examinations separately.

As is often the case of men or institutions confronted with problems of rapid adjustment and the attendant criticism when they fail to meet everyone's expectations, the NCA became increasingly concerned about its public image. In a day when self-promotion had become routine in politics, business, and government, it was inevitable that the Association would respond to the apparent popular misunderstanding of its role by attempting to interpret its program more systematically than had ever seemed necessary before. Over the years the promotion of good public relations had remained more or less hit-or-miss, with the exception of the publication of the *Quarterly*, which had been started in 1927. Valuable as it was as the official voice and news bulletin of the Association, the *Quarterly*'s circulation was limited to the official membership, which was almost entirely institutional; it rarely got into the hands of the public, hardly even into the hands of anyone but administrators of schools and colleges.

For a half dozen years in the late 1940's and early 1950's various proposals for a coordinated public relations policy were considered. A four-page news and information bulletin, *That You May Know Your NCA*, was initiated in 1952; three years later it was retitled *NCA Today*. Designed for a wide distribution over

12. Norman Burns, "Accrediting Enters a New Phase," *NCAQ*, XXVII (January 1953), p. 293.
13. Ewald B. Nyquist, "Life Begins at Forty: A Brief History of the Commission [on Higher Education, Middle States Association of Colleges and Secondary Schools]" (Typed manuscript, 1961); see also Nyquist, "National and Regional Developments in Cooperative Evaluation and Accrediting Activity," *Journal of Engineering Education*, XLIV (May 1964), pp. 533-538.

the NCA area, some 12,000-15,000 copies of each issue were distributed regularly three times during each school year.[14] Meantime, the constitution of the Association was amended in 1954 to give to the Executive Committee the power to "coordinate and publicize the work of the various commissions in such a way as to further most effectively the object of the Association"; the work was put into the hands of a reorganized Committee on Public Relations. Other publicity projects included the production of film strips on the activities of the NCA, a public relations hand book, and a leaflet, "Know Your North Central," which first appeared in 1961.

When Burns became permanent secretary of the Association in 1960, one of the duties included in his office was management of public relations; at the same time, the editorial board of the *Quarterly* and the Committee on Public Relations were combined into a Committee on Publications and Information Service. This decision followed much discussion and the rejection of a minority movement to hire professional publicity personnel. The new committee set out to develop a program of professional caliber. In short order, 60,000 copies of a new information brochure, *Know Your North Central,* were distributed among schools, state legislators, and PTA's, and the *NCA Today* was altered to include special issues on single subjects. Publicity at the annual meetings, usually handled by special personnel, was also expanded through the use of news bulletins, press conferences, publications displays, and so on.

Whatever misgivings there were at first about the value of these measures, making the Association well and favorably known beyond the precincts of its own immediate constituency came to be generally accepted as worth the time and effort involved. And indeed the Association shared the responsibility that had devolved upon the educational establishment generally to satisfy the genuine public concern about educational matters that was mani-

14. Summary of Conference of Executive Committee and the Public Relations Committee with the Administrative Committee and the State Chairmen of the Commission on Secondary Schools, January 14, 1956; "Report Upon Public Relations," 1956-1957; statement on the history of *NCA Today* and *That You May Know Your NCA,* multigraphed, August 1960.

fested in such signs as the regular appearance of education sections in the popular news magazines.

Having to explain its role was a new experience for a body that had for years been able to depend upon general popular understanding and acceptance. Regardless of the subtleties that educational leaders may have had in mind, the public understood broadly that the Association somehow or other kept up standards of the schools. But in the circumstances of such pressures as the nationalization of education through Federal assistance, the demands for relevance to a social revolution, and the discovery of poverty and the disadvantaged, the North Central Association not only had to devise new definitions of its role, but it had to come up with lucid and acceptable explanations as well.

The Association's problem was to persuade a public conditioned to a concept of education defined largely as they knew it in terms of a traditional ideal formed by the more prestigious institutions to accept a new ideal of innovation and adjustment, and with it an Association that was suggesting that it would become an agency of change. The first step in the direction of change and innovation had occurred long before with the adoption of the *Evaluative Criteria,* although at the time the full implications of the move were only imperfectly understood. Despite the countless explanations that qualitative measures had replaced quantitative standards, the definition of an acceptable institution had really changed very little between 1934 and 1955; it remained essentially a copy of a "traditionally prestigious institution,"[15] a product of tradition more than of planning.

This was the situation that the Association set out, in 1963, to remedy. In the words of its leadership, the new role of the Association was to be "Promoting Constructive Changes."[16]

15. Norman Burns, "Changing Concepts of Higher Education," *NCAQ,* XXXVIII (Spring 1964), pp. 296-299; Selden, *Accreditation: A Struggle Over Standards in Higher Education,* p. 43.

16. Edward J. Drummond, *et al.,* "The Role of the North Central Association in Promoting Constructive Changes in Education," *NCAQ,* XXXVII (Fall 1963), pp. 190-204. See also Frank H. Bowles, "The Place of the Regional Association in the Future Educational Scene," *Proceedings, Middle States Association of Colleges and Secondary Schools,* 1957, pp. 24-36.

V

Improving Education Through the Accreditation Process

A. The Commission on Colleges and Universities[1]

The chief source of agitation for a new look in accreditation and Association policies, at least in the early stages of the movement, was the Commission on Colleges and Universities. Dissatisfaction over the failure to implement fully the theories of qualitative evaluation was already considerably advanced in the early 1950's. There were, it seemed to the critics, as many overly detailed forms to complete as ever; moreover there were rising doubts about evaluating institutions from junior college to complex university on a single scale.

As early as 1947, on Norman Burns's suggestion that institutions be grouped by type, that is, on the basis of degrees offered, the Commission instructed the secretary to study the possible effects of such a regrouping on accreditation procedures. From 1952 to 1958 the collection of data from member institutions was discontinued. It was then resumed with some changes until 1961, when it was dropped because it was generally agreed that the information collected indicated very little about an institution's worth.[2] Abandoning statistical measures shifted the weight

1. In 1970, the By-Laws would change the name to Commission on Institutions of Higher Education.
2. Robert F. Sullivan, "Report of the Executive Board [Commission on Colleges and Universities] on Some Basic Policy Considerations," (duplicated, March 1963).

of evaluation from the institutional pattern map, in use since 1934, to the judgment of the examiner or examining committee.

In the meantime, the role of the Commission was subject to much discussion. Burns argued that much more attention should be given to special studies by the Commission, both to determine what the basis of accreditation should be, and to offer some suggestions toward solving basic problems confronting American colleges and universities. He said that carrying on a continuing study of developments in education had been one of the central goals when the qualitative evaluation was started in 1934, but that lack of funds and the mere keeping abreast of applications had prevented much work in such studies. The time had come, he said, when the studies were the "first and greatest need" of the Association. They should deal with the growing diversity among institutions of higher education, with developing methods to encourage individuality as the road to quality, with reconsidering professional and general accrediting, and with finding means to transform the Association into a "force for the advancement of higher education." An immediate necessity, he declared, was the development of a training program for examiners.[3]

His proposals were put into effect within the next few years. But the approach to leadership was never entirely clear in the councils of the Association. At the beginning it appears that there was considerable sentiment for making the NCA and its commissions into active initiatory agencies for innovation and leadership. But by the late 1960's sentiment was shifting once more toward encouraging the institutions themselves to develop new ideas, while concentrating the Association energies on the business of accreditation and examination. In part, at least, the return to the former emphasis came about because these activities had expanded so much that they took up practically all of the time of the Association and of its accrediting commissions.

In the summer of 1953, on Burns's urging, the Commission on

3. See Dewey Stuit, "Accreditation—Its Problems and Its Future," *Teachers College Record*, LXII (May 1961), pp. 629-641.

Colleges and Universities appointed three study committees: the Committee on Reorganization of Accrediting Procedures, the Committee on Planning, and a Committee on Professional Accrediting Problems. Among the basic ideas proposed by these committees was the development of a consultant service to provide expert advice for institutions, accredited or not, that were interested in improving their offerings, and a clearinghouse service to digest and circulate educational studies about the Association.[4]

The Committee on Professional Education proposed that a "generalist" appointed by the North Central Association accompany the examining teams of professional accrediting agencies. Under the plan, which was adopted in 1954, the generalist was to reflect the institutional point of view. He was to use his influence to guard against unreasonable requirements imposed by a professional group intent on advancing its own special interests without sufficient regard for the fact that the professional program with which they were concerned was part of a total institution, and must operate within a framework of institutional policy. The generalist was in no sense engaged in a North Central Association accrediting activity. His presence on the team was merely that of a "friend in court" for the university. Greater attention to local needs and diversity among institutions was to be achieved by dividing the Higher Commission's jurisdiction into five regional districts, each with a committee of its own; the model for this proposal was quite obviously the State Committee system used by the Secondary Commission.

Amendments to the constitution designed to enable the Association to discharge its redefined functions were submitted to the membership in early 1955 and approved at the annual meeting in March. The Association was divided into five districts, and member institutions were grouped by type. The Commission on Colleges and Universities (forty-five members, later increased to fifty-one) was reorganized to include three members elected by

4. Norman Burns, "The New Role of the Commission on Colleges and Universities," *NCAQ*, XXIX (October 1954), pp. 161-166.

the Commission on Secondary Schools and representatives from each district and from each type of institution in the districts. Members were limited to a single four-year term.[5] Doctor's degree-granting institutions in each district were entitled to two commissioners for each ten institutions, with a minimum of one and a maximum of four from each district; the other three types of institutions—those granting M.A.'s, those granting B.A.'s, and junior colleges—in each district were entitled to one commissioner for each ten, with a minimum of one and a maximum of four.

In practice the District Committees became points of local contact more than anything else and without much in the way of specific duties except to nominate members for the Commission. The Committees by Type, on the other hand, became the major reviewing agencies for institutions applying for accreditation, and the initiators of policy for the particular type of institution they represented.[6]

Following a conference of examiners on the subjective nature of qualitative judgments, *The Guide for The Evaluation of Institutions of Higher Education* was issued in 1958. It posed seven basic questions to assist the examiner:

1. Is the educational task of the institution clearly defined?
2. Are the necessary resources available for carrying out the task of the institution?
3. Is the institution well organized for carrying out its educational task?
4. Are the curriculum and instructional programs adapted to goals of the institution?
5. Are conditions of faculty service such as to promote high morale?
6. Is student life on the campus well-balanced and educationally meaningful?

5. Constitution, NCA, Article IV; 1954 By-Laws. The five districts were A (Michigan, Ohio, West Virginia), B (Wisconsin, Illinois, Indiana), C (North Dakota, South Dakota, Nebraska, Minnesota, Iowa), D (Kansas, Oklahoma, Missouri, Arkansas), E (Wyoming, Colorado, New Mexico, Arizona).

6. Editorial, *Journal of Higher Education*, XXVI (June 1955), pp. 332-335; Paul C. Reinert, "The Present Status of Accreditation," *College and University*, XXIX (July 1954), pp. 583-591.

7. Is the level of achievement of students consistent with the goals of the institution?[7]

Thus was begun what Robert Sullivan, associate secretary of the Higher Commission, called the "period of purposes," when purpose became "the primary principle of evaluation."

Improvement meant not only the provision of an examination service for new institutions seeking some mark of official approval, but attention also to the welfare of those that were already members, some of which had come under almost no scrutiny for years. In 1956, the Commission on Colleges and Universities adopted a plan for revisiting all member institutions every ten years. The first visits—twenty-five in 1957—were not entirely satisfactory. No uniform technique had been developed and institutional representatives varied widely in what they expected and in their reactions. Some declared the entire venture was a waste of time, which perhaps it was when a team spent a single day of casual visiting around a campus, as some of them did.

Faculties and administrators of large institutions sometimes resented suggestions from examiners who came from small colleges and *vice versa*. The main difficulty was that the *in toto* examinations were largely conceived in terms of the smaller colleges which could be examined as a whole. A good many of the questions dealing with institutional purpose, teaching load, and the like had little relevance for an institution as complex and varied as a state university. The preliminary self-examinations that were required likewise were clearly better fitted to the small college organization than to the university, where they were likely to be assigned to an administrator or a committee instead of being handled as an all-institution project.

The techniques of evaluation, which continued to be an object of concern, were thoroughly revised in 1961, and again in 1964. Under the new rules institutions now submitted pre-examination "profile" and "basic institutional data" reports, the contents of which were clearly prescribed. Size of teams was also set at from

7. For a discussion and explanation of these guideline questions see Burns, "Accreditation etc." in Fischer and Sweet.

two to four depending on the size of institutions, and length of visit was set at from two to four days. Instructions issued in 1964 advised the teams about whom to visit on a campus, what to look for, and what to include in a report. It was repeatedly emphasized that the purpose of visits was not to uncover reasons to penalize an institution but to give guidance for improvement.[8] The problem of evaluating the "complex university" was partly solved by the decision to abandon the total examination and concentrate on such key functions as the decision-making process, curricular planning and change, faculty recruitment, and admissions. Examinations of any activities not directly involved in the educational process, such as the business office operation, were dropped entirely.

In general the program had won approval by the end of the 1960's, although the problem of assessing reliably the quality of an institution continued to be troublesome, still too subjective for comfort in the sense of its being a product of reputation, general atmosphere, and the predilections of even the trained examiners that the NCA was simultaneously developing. How, for example, did one assess a faculty? Quite clearly, the number of Ph.D.'s was not an infallible guide to quality, but what other tests could be applied? It was necessary also to learn how to assess "the relationship of the dynamics of an administration to educational excellence."

A study of NCA examiners' reports in 1967 (after the Association had a well-established program to choose highly qualified personnel and to train them before sending them out) observed that reports were "notably weak" in comments or evidence on institutional quality as reflected in the achievement of students. The study also criticized excessive attention to the role of administration and insufficient concern for the role of faculty in innovation and decision-making. Long-term planning as a measure of quality and vitality also received much less attention than records of past

8. "The Periodic Membership Review Program" (adopted by the Commission on Colleges and Universities at the annual meeting, 1964), Mimeographed, August 1967.

achievements; in the words of the report, "a good institution should know where it is going."[9]

The immediate effect of the expanded activity and the emphasis upon on-the-spot analysis was to raise a problem of finding or developing additional personnel capable of performing such services. "The abandonment of statistical forms [had] forced the evaluators to derive norms out of their own experience," and such norms were "validated by the Association when it commissioned people to serve as evaluators." In 1955 the Commission began approaching foundations for funds to establish a consultant-examiner training program under the title, "Leadership Training Project." A Carnegie Foundation grant of $147,000 in 1956 launched the program. A supplemental grant of $61,000 was received in 1960, and the NCA undertook to continue the program with its own funds on a limited basis thereafter.

Beginning in 1956 "classes" of fifteen college and university faculty and administrators "showing promise of leadership" were selected from a group nominated by their home institutions. The immediate objective was to supply the Association's continuing need for evaluators and consultants; a secondary objective was to prepare promising people for administrative positions. The latter purpose of the program was discarded by 1963 and appointees, whose designation was changed from fellow to associate, were chosen from the ranks of established administrators and faculty.

The enrollees went through a series of "guided field experiences" in which they had a chance to visit a variety of institutions as members of examining teams. In all, they spent approximately a month during the training year before being officially named consultants. They met three times during the year to discuss their experiences, and also attended a two-week summer workshop.[10] Burns and Allan Pfnister, his assistant secretary, prepared a fifty-

9. Paul L. Dressel, "Some Observations on NCA Examiners Reports," *NCAQ*, XLII (Fall, 1967), pp. 214-219.
10. Allan O. Pfnister, "A Regional Accreditation Agency Experiments in the Training of Consultants for Higher Educational Institutions," *Education Record*, XL (January 1959), pp. 62-68.

seven page study guide detailing what should be included in an examination and how to obtain information and impressions.

In 1962, when the program was in its fifth year, it was estimated that about one hundred examiners and thirty consultants would be needed for the forthcoming NCA examinations, about forty more than were available. Five years later, when the Association had more than two hundred consultant-examiners on hand, the demand was still exceeding the supply. By this time, with foundation funds no longer available, and the need still rising, the program of training was reduced to ten or twelve days throughout the year. Associates also frequently served in the consultant service. Almost from the beginning the service of providing expert consultants for new institutions seeking accreditation or to institutions launching new programs was recognized as one of the most useful functions of the NCA.

Changes in the general procedure of accreditation were considerable. At the March 1961 annual meeting, the Association approved a new policy whereby an institution working toward membership could become a "Candidate for Membership." Eligibility criteria stated that the "institution must be chartered as a nonprofit institution; must include in its curriculum or as a prerequisite for entrance or graduation a sequence of general education; and must be actively engaged in seeking membership in the Association."

An institution which was engaged in a self-study project could submit a "status study" which would contain a complete statement of institutional purposes, a discussion of the key problems that the institution faced, and those data to be used in the preparation of the self-study report. In consideration of the status study, the Commission was concerned with the clarity of the institution's conception of its goals and the level of progress it had achieved in the development of educational standards, facilities, and resources. Candidates, or those planning to apply for candidacy, could request the services of a consultant.

Central to the procedure and one of the innovations of the era of purpose and self-improvement was the submission of a "comprehensive and intensive" self-study report. The Association spent much time in developing directives and forms to assist institutions in making this report. These studies were intended to involve an institution's personnel, faculty, and administration, not only in analyzing their operations but in thinking through their *raison d'être*.[11]

Following the self-study, the Association dispatched an examining team to the institution. The examiners sent a report of their findings to the members of the Commission and the appropriate Committee by Type (of which there were nine in operation after 1964 to represent the four categories of institutions). After a formal hearing for the institution's representatives before the Committee by Type and the chairman or other representatives of the examination team, the committee made recommendations to the Executive Board, which in turn made its own recommendations to the Commission and thence to the Association.

Another kind of status, that of Correspondent, was added in 1967. The need for this classification had arisen from the United States Office of Education request, made in 1964, that the Association provide it with information for its recommendations to the states for allocating Federal funds to institutions under the Higher Education Facilities Act of 1963 (Public Law 88-204). The Association established the policy of limiting such "Approval" to a nonaccredited institution which filed a letter stating intention to begin working toward accreditation and qualifying for Candidate status within two years. Failure to comply meant having Federal funds certification discontinued. After 1965 such institutions were required to accept an Association consultant. By August 1966 the Association had granted such tentative approval to twenty-nine of the thirty institutions in the NCA area which had made application for Federal funds.[12]

In October 1967 the Executive Board of the Commission in-

11. Earland I. Carlson, "Institutional Identity and Self-Study," *NCAQ*, XXXIX (Winter 1965), pp. 263-272.
12. Federation of Regional Accrediting Associations (FRACHE), "Pre-Candidacy Status: Correspondent, Rationale," Mimeographed, October 1967.

stituted the pre-candidacy status entitled "Correspondent," which the U. S. Office of Education accepted as a replacement for "federal fund eligibility approval." The new classification provided an institution with an opportunity to establish a formal, publicly recognized relationship with the Association, and indicated that the institution had given evidence of sound planning, had the resources to implement its plans, and was interested in working toward accreditation. Seventy-two institutions appeared on the first published list of Correspondents in the Summer, 1968 *Quarterly*.

An immediate problem arising from the procedure was that some institutions which had been approved for this limited purpose implied in their public releases and student recruitment literature that they had been accredited. More serious was the danger that the NCA, and the other regional associations which also had similar arrangements with the U. S. Office of Education, could be charged with slipping into a quasi-official relationship with the U.S. Office of Education. This risk was one of which NCA officials were acutely conscious. Yet the work needed doing, and the alternative, if the regional associations failed to respond, was Federal government action, an even greater threat to autonomy.

In the meantime, the rapid development of graduate programs —expansion in established institutions and entirely new programs in former teachers and agricultural colleges—added another dimension to accreditation. A new status accordingly entered the picture; this was preliminary accreditation, which was applied to new graduate programs in NCA member institutions. If the developing graduate school—a new concept in the era of rapid expansion—expanded its programs, as it was very likely to do, the Association sent specialists in the appropriate areas to check on the institution's readiness to make the contemplated moves. Thus new graduate programs in approved institutions were now coming under some systematic supervision and scrutiny. In the days of almost sole attention to accreditation of new institutions, such programs had often emerged with little or no attention from the Association.

Similar problems of expansion and/or improved mobility arose with respect to the appearance of branch campuses, special six-year programs for teachers, and the Master of Arts in Teaching (MAT) degrees, the latter quite frequently in undergraduate liberal arts colleges. The Specialist programs, usually for six years, were established somewhere between the M.A. and the doctorate, sometimes as terminal programs and otherwise as an interim step to the doctorate. These degrees made their appearance in force after the mid-1950's largely in response to a rising chorus of charges that teachers and school administrators were badly prepared for their jobs, having either taken too few of the courses they needed or the wrong ones.[13]

In 1955 the Commission on Colleges and Universities set up a committee to formulate a policy statement on the five-year M.S. in Education and the six-year Specialist programs. An extensive report on NCA policy was adopted and circulated in 1958.[14] It rejected the plausible argument advanced by some academicians that additional undergraduate study to fill in the educational gaps of teachers already holding degrees could properly be counted for credit toward a graduate degree. That is, the integrity of graduate work was to be maintained, but the emphasis upon research training could be cut back to a mere orientation experience.

A parallel development was the rise of self-consciousness about teacher education in the liberal arts colleges. These private colleges, whatever their qualifications for the job in comparison with the public teachers colleges, had always produced a substantial proportion of the classroom teachers in both elementary and high schools, in particular the teachers of the traditional academic subjects. Recognition of this fact and also of the fact that such colleges often failed to do much in the way of specific measures

13. Robert W. McCulloch, "The Role of Graduate Schools in Teacher Education: A study of Ten Graduate Programs," *NCAQ*, XXX (October 1955), pp. 211-218; for a perceptive comment on the aspects of such upward mobility, see Richard W. Burkhardt, "The Teachers College Becomes a University," *NCAQ*, XLI (Winter 1967), pp. 271-278.

14. "Graduate Programs in Education," Mimeographed, March 1958; Allan O. Pfnister, "A Statement on Graduate Study for Teachers and Educational Specialists," *Journal of Teacher Education*, X (March 1959), pp. 16-21.

to train their teachers for their jobs had been the original impetus for the NCA Liberal Arts Project.

The project undoubtedly was one of many factors contributing to a growing introspection on liberal arts college campuses about their hitherto almost ignored role in manning the public schools. Another important influence was the private colleges' search for concrete evidence of their immediate usefulness in the increasingly stiff competition with the frequently better-financed public institutions.

Probably the factor of most importance in the colleges' concern was their enlisting in the expanding debate between "educationists" and "subject matter" specialists over the proper content of teacher education. Concern over goals was intensified by the appearance of substantial Federal funds for teacher education and by the efforts of the newly formed National Council for the Accreditation of Teacher Education to develop a body of uniform requirements for training teachers. The colleges, many of which had small-scale M.A. programs dating from years back, programs that were usually in decline, found a chance to revive them and to take a stand for subject-matter teacher education when the Master of Arts in Teaching programs put in their appearance in the 1950's. When Federal funds became available for summer teachers' institutes, first in the sciences and later for other subjects, the advocates of reviving M.A. programs were able to obtain the necessary funds to support them.

The Commission on Colleges and Universities had given tentative approval to the MAT programs as early as 1954, when state colleges in Oklahoma had established them. A more complex problem arose in 1960 when Carleton College, which had no graduate program at all, received a contract for summer science institutes from the National Science Foundation. The college requested permission to offer graduate credit which could be transferred to degree programs in graduate schools, because it had no intention of developing a full program of its own. The Association had no wish to discourage the development of summer programs in colleges like Carleton, but technically the college, a very good one, was not accredited for M.A. work, nor did the college wish such approval. On the other hand, the NCA did not accredit single course offerings. After much discussion, the Commission offered the tentative suggestion that colleges solve such problems by prior arrangements with graduate institutions to get courses accepted.[15]

As has been pointed out above, the Commission rejected the notion, which had considerable currency, especially among the liberal arts colleges, that MAT programs merely filled in the gaps of an inadequate undergraduate education—that is, that they were not graduate programs at all. As the Commission viewed the matter, a substantial part of any programs culminating in the Master's degree, whatever their title or intent, had to be on a graduate level if they were to be accredited.

Branch campuses or off-campus programs of established institutions were yet another phenomenon for which the accrediting associations had no precedent for guidance. By the middle 1960's huge numbers of students were being educated in these centers; for example, in 1965 over 66,000 such students were enrolled in branches in Illinois, which had the largest number of these programs in off-campus locations in the Association area; there were nearly a quarter million in the entire nineteen-state NCA region. Forty-one percent of NCA institutions had extension programs ranging from a single two-hour evening course taught in a high school building to university centers offering advanced degrees. Thirty-six institutions had programs in 95 foreign countries involving nearly 4,000 students.

The Association first took official note of the off-campus development in 1956 when the Executive Board (then Board of Review) of the Commission devoted part of its summer meeting to discussing their implications for accreditation. A committee appointed for the purpose developed a statement of policy in 1958. There the matter rested, except for some periodic expressions of unease, for another five years because the Association had nei-

15. Albert J. Huegli, *et al.,* "Graduate Programs for Liberal Arts Colleges," *NCAQ,* XLI (Spring 1967), pp. 316-325.

ther the funds nor the personnel to give every branch a full accreditation examination. At its November meeting in 1963 the
Executive Board directed that "an effort be made" to include the
centers in review visits in the following spring. A year later the
1958 policy statement was re-examined and the Board agreed to
survey the situation to determine the size of the problem; in the
meantime it agreed on some preliminary policies.

A full statement of policy on accrediting off-campus programs
and branches was issued in 1965 and revised in 1968. Limited
programs of a few courses were to remain under the status of the
parent institution. But operationally separate branches, or centers
that were in effect separate, were to be accredited as independent
institutions without regard to the extent of control from the parent. They were grouped in a separate listing of accredited colleges for the first time in 1969. The Association had probably
furthered separatist tendencies among university branches, and
had thereby set the stage for a sharp increase in the number of
independent higher educational institutions.

On the other hand, off-campus programs in foreign countries
were continued under the parent institutions' accreditation status.
But the Board suggested in 1965 when it was settling on its off-
campus institution policies that a separate statement of policy
would eventually be necessary. A portent of even larger problems
to come was the request that same year from the Sorbonne for
accreditation for a Master of Arts program in French specifically
designed for American students. The Commission on Colleges
and Universities' reply to that august institution, the mother of
the British and American university tradition, was that it could
seek preliminary accreditation for its program by following the
usual procedures outlined in NCA statements of policy.

Most of the expansion discussed thus far was not entirely unfamiliar. It reflected the upward movement and growth of established four-year institutions that had always been a part of the
American educational scene, although at a somewhat more deliberate and predictable pace than that of the 1950's and 1960's.
A much less familiar expansion was that developing on the lower
side of the collegiate system. Even here, there were elements of

familiarity in the conventional junior colleges existing largely to prepare students for entrance into four-year colleges or to provide a minimal general education program and a terminal degree (usually the Associate of Arts) for students who lacked the abilities or the desire to go further.

However, new kinds of post-high school institutions, community colleges providing terminal programs, or vocational/technical institutes, were developing rapidly. A great many, aimed at the very students who had found literature and allied subjects beyond their capacities or interests in high school, made no effort to meet the NCA requirement for a liberal arts core, even to the extent of staying within the flexible rule that it merely be "appropriate" to the institution's purpose. By 1960 there were 800,000 students in the junior colleges of the nation, 25 percent more than only two years before. About one eighth of them were in the NCA area attending about two hundred junior and technical colleges, of which only seventy-one were accredited. Moreover, the period of expansion had only really begun, because the United States Government's "war on poverty" educational programs were just then getting under way.[16]

Already faced with more accrediting work than it could handle efficiently, the Commission on Colleges and Universities attempted for a time to continue with its established definitions and policies. But by the late 1960's the NCA had to turn its attention to the new phenomenon.[17] An entire new area of education was developing; it would either develop its own rationale and standards as a separate system, or it could be incorporated into the American system that had been developed by the voluntary regional associations. The latter was not only desirable for the associations, but it was desired by a substantial number of the new institutions. The American Association of Junior Colleges (AAJC), itself under pressures to permit piecemeal accreditation of vocational programs, was pressing the NCA to readjust its standards to include a broadening of the general education defini-

16. Figures from the Directory of the Office of Health, Education, and Welfare, reported in *NCAQ*, XXXVI (Spring 1962), pp. 309-310.

17. Raymond J. Young, "Crucial Times for North Central Area Junior College Development," *NCAQ*, XXXVI (Spring 1962), pp. 323-327.

tions and the recognition of technical and vocational programs.

The two problems that the Association struggled with the most were the formulation of a satisfactory definition of what a junior college was and the rationalization of technical education, with liberal arts programs much curtailed, as collegiate level education. The first was resolved in 1965 by a statement to the effect that a community junior college must have a jurisdiction and faculty clearly separated from any local high school. In 1950 when the question of dealing with special institutions—which could include anything from business schools to art institutes, theological seminaries, or schools of cosmetology—came up, the Board of Review ruled that no institution without an acceptable general education program need even apply and that such institutions as had been accepted earlier would have three years in which to add the programs. The ruling was reaffirmed in 1956, again in 1957, and once more in 1958 following a study of the problem by a committee appointed for the purpose.[18]

Pressure to assume a more flexible and realistic position continued to rise as the number of vocational and technical schools increased, and in 1965 Burns offered a solution in line with the NCA's own professed position: that such institutions be considered in terms of their own announced purposes and philosophy. Burns argued too that the NCA would thereby not even be making much of a change from what it was already doing in fact because even in such vocational institutions as had been accredited, the NCA had no way of ensuring that students actually took the general education courses that the schools were required to offer in order to be accredited. The most urgent arguments, however, were that the institutions were growing rapidly, that they would expand even more with Federal funds available to them, and that the Association had better take advantage of what was still a receptive attitude in the AAJC to use NCA influence to guide their development into desirable channels.

Three years later an *ad hoc* committee of the Commission on

18. Norman Burns, "Accrediting and Educational Diversity," *NCAQ*, XXXV (April 1961), pp. 257-258.

Colleges and Universities appointed to study the question of accrediting non-degree granting vocational and technical schools recommended unanimously that the Association set up guidelines to be used by both accrediting commissions (it specifically rejected any consideration of establishing another commission for the new schools) for the "evaluation of vocational and technical programs of less than the associate-degree level." Final recommendations from the two commissions were to be presented to the NCA Board of Directors at the annual meeting in 1969. These actions were a vote once more for the ever-widening variety and flexibility in American education. Movements for coordinating the accreditation of vocational-technical education throughout the country were also under way in the Federation of Regional Accrediting Commissions of Higher Education and the National Commission on Accrediting.

One more area of educational expansion—and of concern in the Association—was the proprietary school; such institutions were appearing in increasing numbers. The NCA was under some pressure to undertake their evaluation in the 1960's, but the Executive Board of the Higher Commission rejected the idea in 1962—somewhat tentatively—on the grounds that the Association already had undertaken as much work as it could handle.

Perhaps the most conspicuous single aspect of the Association's history in the 1960's was an accelerating activity to match the feverish growth of the American educational enterprise. In 1967 forty-seven institutions, varying in style and purposes from the Arkansas Art Center, the Area Ten Community College (Iowa), to Oral Roberts University, were listed as Correspondents, which is to say that all were in some stage of preparing for accreditation and therefore requiring attention and assistance from the Association. In addition, the Association was preparing new institutions for their first steps toward Correspondent status, examining others for final approval, conducting the regular ten-year reviews of its members institutions, and examining and advising on off-campus centers and new graduate programs.

In order to manage its affairs with improved efficiency, the

Commission on Colleges and Universities was reorganized and enlarged in 1955; a further expansion of the Board and Commission to include representatives of the post high school vocational schools was adopted at the 1969 annual meeting. In 1964 the number of the Committees by Type was increased to nine. A second annual meeting of the Commission to consider accreditation reports had to be added in midsummer in order to keep up with accreditation activities.

Annual dues were set in 1967 at $200 for junior colleges and ranged upward for each level to a maximum of $600 for the Ph.D.-granting university. The accreditation and review activities, however, cost more money than the annual dues and the relatively low examination fee structure could provide. Fees for an accreditation examination or the once-in-ten-year review visit increased from $1200 in 1963 to $1600 in 1969 for two-year and four-year colleges and were graduated upward to a charge of $2400 in 1963 and $3600 in 1969 for a Ph.D.-granting university.

Although various critics from time to time voiced doubts that Association membership was worth the expense, no institutions chose to risk resignation. Moreover, removal from the accredited list could be disastrous, as was demonstrated when Parsons College lost its accredited status in the summer of 1967. No action of the Association, not even its victory in the Langer case in 1938, attracted the public attention that attended the Parsons College "case"—the second expulsion from the Association to come before the courts.

The difference in the issues involved in the two cases is marked. In the Langer case the offense was a governor's interference in the internal affairs of a college, a clearly defined problem on which the Association position had been unequivocal almost from its founding. In the Parsons case the Association acted because the internal administration of a college had failed to maintain the standard of academic integrity required for membership in the Association.

For the purposes of this history it is necessary only to relate the essential outlines of the action and to point to its significance. (The full story is long and complex, and would require a chapter in itself.) Parsons was a small, moderately old (for the Midwest), and unprosperous college in the small town of Fairfield in southeastern Iowa. It was nearly bankrupt and its enrollment down to about two hundred in 1948 when it was first disaccredited —with almost no attention attracted by the event. Its standing in the Association was restored in 1950, although many of its problems, chiefly related to inadequate financial support, still remained unsolved. Then prosperity struck almost overnight, after a dynamic minister-promoter-president, Millard G. Roberts, arrived on the scene in 1955. From then on the college's history was spectacular.

Roberts made Parsons into the proving ground for two ideas, which he advertised far and wide as the answer to two of the most plaguing problems in higher education. One, in the area of educational theory, was that a substantial number of college dropouts were not necessarily incompetent, but were mainly the victims of unsuitable teaching or professors' indifference. Parsons was to become an institution of second chance which would educate the dropout by special teaching techniques. The other idea, in the area of institutional management, was that the chief reason for colleges' financial difficulties and eternal dependence upon gifts or taxes for support was inefficiency and underuse of their faculties and resources. Again by revolutionizing its methods and installing efficient managerial procedures, Parsons proposed to pay its way and even turn a profit, all out of the fees collected from its second-chance students. None of this would be at the cost of trimming quality; Parsons would offer the best level of education that money could buy by paying the highest salaries in the nation to secure the ablest professors there were.

And it seemed to work. An enrollment increase to about 5,000 students in only a few years and a new campus that literally dwarfed the old one added to Roberts's formidable abilities as an advertiser and promoter. The overnight material success attracted national attention. Many communities with a struggling college on their hands, or ambitious to get a college started, were persuaded that a solution to the financing problem had been found. Roberts actively encouraged them and even lent personnel from his college and financial assistance—nearly a half million dollars in all—out of his own "profits." The latter gesture was impressive indeed.

However, no colleges of any standing followed Parsons's example, although a good many of them were facing increasing financial stringencies. Whatever influence the Parsons example may have had was perhaps to encourage more efficient use of resources, although the Roberts idea of spreading out the resources of his "star" faculty through the extensive use of para-teaching personnel also found few converts; the universities were already doing this with graduate assistants to the point of diminishing returns, and the chief *raison d'être* of the private colleges was that they did not do this sort of thing at all.

The North Central Association adopted a prudent waiting attitude, although some of its members were impatient for action against what they regarded as a fraudulent operation. It was not until 1963, following the receipt of serious charges against the college administration from the Parsons faculty, that an NCA team investigated the college. Its report listed seven major points of criticism, and the Commission then placed the college on probation for a year and scheduled a full accreditation examination to be concluded before the annual meeting in the spring of 1964.

In due course another NCA team reexamined the college, and on its recommendation the Executive Board and the Commission voted successively to "remove probationary status with the provision that an NCA consultant be appointed and a review be made within three years." The scheduled visit was made in February 1967, and was concluded with the recommendation that the college be continued in "a sort of provisional status [of accreditation], subject to conditions agreed to by the College, but short of formal probation." The Executive Board rejected the proposal, however, and recommended that Parsons be dropped from membership for "persistent failure on the part of the College to correct serious weaknesses in its operation and the Executive Board's lack of confidence in the administrative leadership of the College." The issue, as the Association leadership had come to view it after frequent examinations, was that the college administration was both unable and unwilling to perform the educational services that it had advertised far and wide. At the annual business meeting, April 6, 1967, the assembled membership of the Association approved the Board's decision without discussion. The effective date of disaccreditation was set for June 30, 1967.[19]

When the college turned to the courts with the plea that Association action would bring irreparable harm to the institution and that it had been denied due process in the Association proceedings, the college again lost its case. In the opinion of the court, ruling on a plea for preliminary injunction, due process was not involved because the North Central Association was a voluntary body, in no sense an arm of government. One of the precedents cited in support of the decision was the Langer case of a generation before.[20] In a vain effort to forestall the final decision, the college's board of trustees dismissed the president before the ruling became final.

The consequences for Parsons College could hardly have been more dramatic. Registration in September 1967 fell to less than half the figure of the preceding fall, a substantial number of the faculty left, and the dazzling salaries of those who remained were reduced by two-thirds or more. Moreover, the sound business practices of which President Roberts had made so much were revealed to have left the college with a crushing debt of about $14,000,000. Quite possibly, in view of the financial situation of the institution, its collapse was inevitable, regardless of what ac-

19. *Parsons College, etc., Plaintiff v. North Central Association of Colleges and Secondary Schools,* Civil Action No. 67 C 1109, U.S. District Court, Northern District of Illinois, Eastern Division, Memorandum of Decision with Respect to the Motion of the Plaintiff for Preliminary Injunction, July 26, 1967.

20. *Ibid.* See also William A. Kaplin and J. Philip Hunter, "The Legal Status of the Educational Accrediting Agency: Problems in Judicial Supervision and Governmental Regulation," *Cornell Law Quarterly,* LII (1966), pp. 104-131.

tion the Association took, but to most observers the direct relationship between the Association's action and the fall of Parsons
College was unmistakable. Under new leadership Parsons College
is now working to regain its accredited status.

The relative infrequency of a situation in which a college or
university's deficiencies lead to the last resort of disaccreditation
had much to do with the publicity which the case received. Far
more normal, and in constant operation, was the quiet, deliberate
procedure of conferences, advice, and adjustment whenever an
institution was being pressed to elevate its standards or to desist
from a questionable practice. Even the new state-wide superboards of higher education, which could conceivably have been a
threat too large for the voluntary association to handle, fell into
the pattern.

Such boards did, however, occasion some adjustments in NCA
policies. Until comparatively recent years, the Association had
more or less limited its direct relationships to college and university governing boards to a polite and informal interview or lun-
cheon on the occasion of an accreditation or review examination.
It was well understood, however, that the NCA stood firmly
against boards' interfering in the internal governance of an institution. The only exceptions to this policy, and this too was in the
process of correction in the mid-1960's, were certain colleges,
controlled by churches or religious orders, wherein the personnel
of boards, administrations, and even faculty overlapped. But the
superboards were designed to intervene because their very purpose was to secure uniformity in a system, to prevent costly du-
plications, or to develop needed educational services. Moreover,
by virtue of their size and their large delegated powers, such
boards were in a position to offer considerable resistance to the
Association if they should choose to do so. Not infrequently,
whether by design or because of the chances for such oversights
in a huge operation, a superboard might authorize the institutions it controlled to launch new programs without following the
procedures of the Association.

In 1965, following a series of conferences with the Director and Chancellor of the Ohio Board of Regents, the Higher Commission clarified the procedures for launching new programs (these applied, of course, to individual institutions as well) by requiring that all responsible state agencies must first authorize a new program before the Association; that is to say, programs in the planning stage would not be approved. Moreover, the NCA has continued its practices of dealing only with individual institutions directly, not through a board of a state system.

In a sense the Parsons case or the problems of governing boards' improper interference are old-fashioned and generally on the decline. Even the superboard could not be viewed as a threat to educational standards; its appearance was usually a mark of maturity in a state's system of higher education and signified the achievement of standards considerably beyond the minimum requirements of the NCA. In the case of Parsons College, the failures were largely those of the president, and they were the customary sort associated with the promoter-president, who has a long and frequently productive history in higher education. The considerable tolerance for Roberts's activities was due to the well-known fact—in educational circles at least—that men like him, rather than faculties, have been the main innovators in higher education; he had arrived on the scene at the very time that the NCA was actively trying to encourage innovation in its member institutions. Roberts's mistake was that he had overstepped the line between what is well conceived and effective innovation and what is not. Most presidents and boards have come to understand the limitation, and major transgressions from either party are now the exception rather than the rule.

In fact, the kind of situation that had developed at Parsons had become essentially a hazard only of the small colleges. Being relatively compact and often administratively centralized, they are vulnerable to large swings in policy that could only rarely occur in the complex university, particularly as they may become increasingly desperate in the search for a uniqueness which will hopefully put them ahead in the race for funds and students. The complex university, usually relatively secure in its situation, has in its very complexity a number of built-in internal controls that provide a large measure of protection from aberration or adventurism.

More serious than the kind of familiar problems that presidents or boards could create on occasion was the increasing possibility that two other parties to the academic enterprise—the faculties and students—would create situations affecting an institution's purposes, its standards, its methods, and hence its accreditation. In addition, the intrusion of pressing contemporary social issues into the academic scene brought into question the view that the college was an ivory tower for intellectual contemplation rather than the arena for social action. The fact that American colleges had always, in theory as well as in practice, gloried in their role of instruments for social improvement meant that there could be no easy resolution of the directions higher education should take in the ferment of the 1960's.

B. The Commission on Secondary Schools

In many respects the history of the Commission on Secondary Schools parallels that of the Commission on Colleges and Universities. A number of changes in procedures and expectations in accreditation quite clearly were inspired by what had been done in the college organization. Such were the renewed emphasis upon qualitative evaluation, the installation of a periodic review program for the entire membership, and a training period for school examiners. The Higher Commission was also the source of most official pronouncements on the need to promote change in the educational system.

But in the actual implementation of such change, the high schools and their Commission clearly moved into the lead. Despite what the Higher Commission spokesmen might propose, the colleges and universities under their supervision changed only moderately. Anyone visiting the average university campus in 1940 and again in 1965 would have found no startling differences in the general conceptions of what education should include or how it should be carried on; the differences were largely physical—improved or even luxurious facilities and bigger enrollments. But also, by the latter date the colleges were, underneath the traditional facades, alive with demands for reform from both students and faculties. (The role of the NCA in this climate of campus activism will be touched upon later.)

The situation was different in the high schools. And the Secondary Commission, with some hesitation at first, to be sure, would move ahead of its sister organization to encourage innovation in the educational process itself. The fact that the NCA had over the years managed to develop an especially strong position meant that its influence would also be substantial. (It may be noted that state departments of education in the regions of NCA jurisdiction have tended to be less fully developed than they are in the other five accrediting associations.)[1]

L. A. Van Dyke, chairman of the Commission on Secondary Schools, writing in a *Quarterly* symposium in 1963, warned the Commission that it must take the initiative in reforming the schools or lose its influence. Van Dyke emphasized that "the big question facing this and other accrediting associations is not whether schools meet certain traditional standards but whether we can adapt our standards and procedures rapidly enough to meet the needs of member schools." The chairman of the Commission on Research and Service put it even more plainly:

> If the North Central Association is to be a positive force for educational improvement, one of the requirements is that it must continually examine its standards in the light of changing needs in education, and in the light of our growing understanding of what makes for good education. This will require the development of an on-going, systematically conducted program of continuing studies of high schools and colleges. . . .
>
> The guidelines of the future will give more attention to what we now call the intangibles . . . such things as institutional atmosphere or climate, the forces of various kinds that are operative relationships.[2]

These statements were in sharp contrast to what would have been said about the role of the Commission no more than a couple of decades earlier. Then, despite gestures toward the school's responsibilities to "this changing world," high school accreditation had continued to be based on more or less fixed standards.[3] The fact that the statements quoted were made when the high school membership was growing substantially and only a short

1. James Bryant Conant, *Shaping Educational Policy* (New York: McGraw-Hill, 1964), pp. 30-31.

2. Edward J. Drummond, L. A. Van Dyke, Herbert Schooling, and Norman Burns, "The Role of the North Central Association in Promoting Constructive Changes in Education," *NCAQ*, XXXVIII (Fall 1963), pp. 190-204.

3. Maynard D. Cochrane, "A Critical Analysis of Changes from 1950 through 1964 in the Policies and Criteria for Approval of Secondary Schools in the North Central Association of Colleges and Secondary Schools," (Ph.D. dissertation, University of Wyoming, 1964), p. 20.

time after a major revision of the *Evaluative Criteria* adds force to the concern they expressed.

The immediate tasks before the Association were outlined in an article published in the *Quarterly* in 1962 as: (1) improving the coordination of high school programs among the states of the Association and among the regional associations; (2) articulating high school and college programs; (3) protecting the schools from the "whims of pressure groups"; (4) drawing upon the findings of research groups and other educational bodies for ideas to improve secondary education; and (5) developing measures to encourage experimentation in the schools themselves.[4]

John Goodlad, a professor of education at UCLA, speaking before the Commission at the annual meeting of 1966, urged that the university laboratory schools be turned back to their original purpose which was to develop and try out new educational ideas and procedures. He deplored the fact that they were either being abandoned altogether or had deteriorated to mere practice-teaching stations for student teachers.

Indeed, by the early 1960's experimentation and reform were already well advanced in the high schools. Less conspicuous than events on the university scene dramatized as they were by the loud exchanges of student protest the changes in secondary education were more concrete. They included such reforms as team teaching, language laboratories, employment of teacher aides, educational TV, honors programs, advanced placement courses, and SAT examinations. It was the era of the new math, conceptual approaches in the social sciences, and modular scheduling. A good many of these were hardly less mysterious to many teachers and administrators than they were to the general public, yet they were perhaps changing American secondary education more profoundly than the controversial progressive ideas had done a generation or more before.

James B. Conant's *The American High School Today*, which was published in 1959, was a considerable factor in the pace of

4. L. A. Van Dyke, "Time for Reappraisal," *NCAQ*, XXXVII (Fall 1962), pp. 163-165.

change. It also defined the lines of a developing controversy about the goals and direction of secondary education in America. Whether he intended it to be so or not, the former president of Harvard was charged with giving far too much attention to the academically talented students—about 15 percent of the high school enrollment—and neglecting the vast majority in a secondary system which was required to accept all comers. In any case, Conant's solution to the problem of teaching all levels of students in the all-purpose high school was ability-grouping. This would in fact become almost a general rule of organization in the 1960's.

Whatever overtones of indifference to the least able portion of the high school population one might read into Conant's report, the schools continued or redoubled their efforts to educate everyone; the advanced-placement courses for the elite were matched by growing attention to reading improvement and counseling, both of which had a long history of sponsorship by the NCA and would be reinforced, along with a host of other measures, by the anti-poverty programs of the Johnson administration's Great Society. However dogmatic Conant may have appeared to some, he recognized the fluidity of the situation and the absence of easy answers and firm guidelines, hence in his words "the importance of experimentation and the desirability of innovation in all phases of education."

In many respects, too, the high schools were more immediately affected by the social ferment of the 1950's and 1960's than the colleges. With the exception of a few notorious episodes like those surrounding the efforts of Autherine Lucy to enter the University of Alabama and James Meredith to enter the University of Mississippi, the bitterest integration battles and by far the most numerous were being fought around the public neighborhood schools. They were vulnerable to all the tensions and fears that the race issue could arouse in a locally controlled institution.

Integration was only one of a bundle of educational and social problems that had given special meaning to the term "urban high school" by the 1960's; these were the "blackboard jungles"—as many sheltered people saw them—of the culturally and emotionally disadvantaged, the poor, and the antisocial, all of them associated with decay of the "inner city" and "flight to the suburbs." For the NCA, as well as for educational organizations and thoughtful leaders everywhere, the situation called for new departures from the traditionally acceptable high school programs that had for years provided college entrance preparation for some without regard to whether they could ever be able or willing to go, vocational training for others with insufficient attention to the state of the job market, and detention for the rest.

The response of the Commission, which also had before it the example of the Higher Commission's reorganization, was to undertake two major revisions of its *Policies and Criteria* for evaluating secondary schools, one in 1960 and a second in 1968. In the first the Commission more or less paralleled the college revision of a few years before in attempting to complete the shift from the old quantitative standards for measuring schools. In the *Policies and Criteria for the Approval of Secondary Schools* of 1959-1960 a section titled "Evaluation of the Composite Effectiveness of Schools" set out to describe quality in terms of an overall individuality and service relative to a specific community climate and need. An element of flexibility was a provision that a school could be classified as "accredited-advised" if it were deficient in one criterion but otherwise sound.

Criteria for accreditation were divided into measures of acceptability (i.e., enough to be accredited) and measures of progress; the latter were described as "additional standards of excellence which a member school is expected to meet within an agreed period of time." (This was the first step toward the periodic seven-year revisitation program which would be inaugurated in 1965.) There were also nine basic guides for an educational program and specific requirements for an acceptable offering—no fewer than twenty-six units, including language arts (four units), science (four), mathematics (four), social studies (four), fine arts two), practical arts (five), health and physical education (one), and foreign language (two effective in 1963). The size of faculty, formerly set at a minimum of one more than the number of years of the school's program in each department, was put at adequate for the curriculum offered, the total enrollment, and the special needs of the pupils and the community.

Extra-classroom activities received extended attention with suggestions for firmer control over interscholastic activities than before, and there were also new sections on guidance and health and safety services. The spirit of the new criteria was clear in the changes made under the head of evaluation. Where formerly six specific objectives had been listed, there was now only a brief statement instructing each member school to "make a planned and continuous evaluation of the effectiveness of its educational program in accomplishing the objectives or outcomes upon which its staff and board have agreed."

These evaluation requirements remained substantially unchanged except for minor revisions until 1969. There was considerable alteration, however, in the general orientation and procedures of the Commission in order to accommodate for new thinking and new problems. The days when the NCA could use the same set of policies and procedures for a decade or more had ended; the cycle of revision was accelerating. Only two years after the 1960 policies were put into effect the Commission began a long-range study to improve its means for "working closely with member schools in each state, stepping up . . . activities in the field of educational research and experimentation, gearing . . . accrediting procedures to media, and seeking to adapt . . . criteria to qualitative factors in education."

In 1962 a series of state-level conferences of member schools was held to consider plans to articulate high school and college programs, to develop effective methods for applying the *Evaluative Criteria,* to consider such matters as flexible scheduling and the attendant matters of teaching load and length of class periods, and to discuss the accreditation of junior high schools. Other projects on the agenda of these meetings were a proposal to shorten the detailed reports required of the high schools and consideration of the use of data-processing equipment to check such reports as were required. It was anticipated that the irksome and sometimes meaningless formal annual reports, a cause of considerable complaint from high schools well above the minimal requirements for accreditation, would be replaced in due time by periodic revisitations by Commission teams interested as much or more in assisting schools in continued improvement as in the bare bones of minimal accreditation.

This was an ambitious program, considerably beyond the financial and personnel resources of the Commission as it was then organized. The Commission's new secretary, Gordon Cawelti, was appointed (June 1962), and the Commission offices moved to Chicago.[5] Cawelti promptly took up quarters in the Shoreland Hotel, thereby essentially completing the centralization of the Association offices and activities. The Commission on Research and Service continued under the old system of an elective volunteer secretary with offices and records outside the central organization.

No small factor in the decision to appoint a young, aggressive secretary for the Secondary Commission was the contrast between the not always certain leadership of this Commission and the vigorous role that Norman Burns played in the Higher Commission and in the Association. The state chairmen and the selection committee specifically insisted on the qualities of leadership and originality among the main requirements for the appointee; he was to develop "challenging forward steps" for the improvement of secondary education, and to work actively with his counterparts in the other regional associations. Practical experience in secondary school administration was another requirement.

Some indication of the stepped-up pace Cawelti would bring to the Commission appeared in his report of 1963. In his first year in office he had begun to work with Secondary Commissions of the other regional associations, had begun working with the American Library Association to develop a reliable method for evaluating libraries, and had met with the National Association of Secondary School Principals to discuss the special problems of the large city high school. Preliminary discussions of a revisita-

5. Cawelti resigned in 1969 and was succeeded by John Stanavage of Cleveland, Ohio.

tion program for the members of the Association had also been held.

Developing the details of the revisitation program, which had been recommended at the annual meeting of state chairmen in the fall of 1962, became the assignment of a new Committee on Accreditation Procedures. On March 31, 1965, a seven-year cycle of revisiting every accredited high school in the Association was begun. In the official words of the Commission, the step was intended.

> . . . to stimulate schools toward school improvement, and to aid in shifting emphasis from detailed, quantitative criteria to more observation of the quality of a program, each member school shall be re-evaluated at least once every seven years, using the materials of the evaluative criteria or some other instrument approved by the Secondary Commission. These materials should be used on a study basis, followed by a visiting NCA Committee of sufficient size that will stay a sufficient length of time to observe all phases of the school's program. A school may also meet this requirement by presenting in writing evidence of having developed its own comprehensive and continuous evaluation program, and by having it reviewed by a visiting NCA Committee, provided that prior permission has been obtained from both the state committee concerned and the Commission on Secondary Schools.[6]

Revisitation meant in effect that periodic self-evaluations would become mandatory for accredited schools. Heretofore, only applicants for accreditation had been required to make such studies, although there was a growing trend for accredited as well as nonaccredited institutions to employ private consultants to analyze their operations. However expert consultant studies might be, they had the disadvantage of depriving faculties and administrations of the experience of carrying through a self-analysis, one of the most important elements in the Association's rationale for the practice.

Preparations for the new program, which would be dependent

6. *NCAQ*, XXXIX (Spring 1965), p. 297.

upon the Association's own personnel and which was expected at the same time to infuse a real change of spirit among the member high schools, were complex and detailed. An "Evaluation Guide for Secondary Schools" (later retitled "Procedures For Evaluation of Secondary Schools") was prepared and published in the *Quarterly*, and a series of special articles described trends and practices in secondary schools for the guidance of the examiners who would be drawn from the ranks of public school administrations and faculties. Dues were raised from $25 to $35 per year in 1962 and to $50 in 1966 to finance the expanded programs.

An important accompaniment of the drive for continued upward progress and individualistic quality was the encouragement of experimentation and innovation in the schools. There was increasing concern that the practice of accreditation encouraged conformity and discouraged unorthodoxy, thereby abandoning the field of ideas to the university academics, the textbook companies, or such special interest groups as were interested in selling materials or promoting a point of view. The Commission and its new secretary wanted to encourage the working members of the Association, the administrators and teachers in the schools not only to accept and try out new ideas, but to think for themselves.

Provision to permit experimentation by waiving strict requirements temporarily had existed since the 1940's, but it was not really until the 1950's that much of an effort was made to encourage experimentation. Although a substantial number of trial programs was permitted over the years, they tended to deal mainly with such details as changing the length of class periods. Nor was much effort made to disseminate information about them and possibly to make them the basis of general reforms. Yet, however modest and even discouraging the immediate response, the steady increase of experimentation could be viewed as a hopeful sign. Nearly forty proposals, more than in any previous year, were approved by the state committees in 1963.[7]

7. Stephen A. Romine, "The Role of the NCA Secondary Commission in Stimulating Experimentation," *NCAQ*, XXXIX (Fall 1964), pp. 204-206; J. Lloyd Trump, "The Experiments We Need." *Ibid.*, pp. 207-209; Gordon

Not content with merely encouraging the schools to seek new paths of learning, the Commission set up its own subcommittee in 1966 to develop new lines of action. This move was in contrast to a simultaneous inclination in the Higher Commission to shift from undertaking experimental measures itself to encouraging its member institutions to take the initiative. The Commission on Secondary Schools took another step forward when, with financial support from the Kettering Foundation's Institute for the Development of Educational Activity (IDEA), it undertook to make a National Innovation Inventory. The other Associations cooperated, and Cawelti directed the project.

Results were published in special editions of *NCA Today* and *Nation's Schools* in 1967.[8] Twenty-seven innovations were tabulated and described from the reports of 7,237 schools. Among these were PSSC Physics, humanities courses, television instruction, games simulation, flexible scheduling, para-professional teaching assistants, student exchanges, optional attendance, and independent learning. The study identified the high schools which had an unusual record for innovation, and provided details on how institutions and groups of teachers actually went about trying out new programs. This down-to-earth descriptive account of what was going on and how to set about doing something was a hard-headed innovation in its own way; this time busy teachers had something more to go on than high-minded and well-intentioned admonitions to be experimental and creative with no hints as to what this might mean.

Many of these innovations were in the direction of improved articulation of high school and college curricula. Procedures in the high schools were increasingly like those of the colleges, and the division between the two was decreased even more by ad-

---

Cawelti, "Stimulating Improvement in Secondary Schools," *NCAQ*, XXXVIII (Spring 1963), pp. 283-284.

8. "Innovative Study of Nation's High Schools Reveals Important Changes in Recent Years," *NCA Today*, XI (March 1967, special issue); and "National Innovation Study Indicates on School Weaknesses," (*NCA Today*, May 1967, special issue). Gordon Cawelti, *et al.*, "Special Study: How High Schools Innovate," *Nation's Schools* (April 1967).

vanced placement programs, the waiving of requirements by colleges, and the installation of college-style courses (the humanities programs, for example) in the high schools. The relaxation of the Carnegie unit requirements in favor of flexible scheduling (officially sanctioned in the *Policies and Criteria* approved for the fall of 1969), the employment of nonprofessional study hall supervisors, and relieving teachers of irksome police and supervisory duties, all were giving to high school teachers some of the freedoms enjoyed by college faculty. At the same time, the relaxation of close all-day supervision was giving high school students something like a college experience.

On the matter of Civil Rights, the Association gradually moved forward with the times, from the Human Relations in the Classroom project, dating back a number of years, to selecting "Human Relations in a Restive Society" as the theme for the annual meeting in 1964. One of the earliest of the desegregation confrontations precipitated in the public schools by the Supreme Court decision of 1954 occurred in member schools of the NCA in Little Rock, Arkansas, in 1958. Acting with great circumspection, the Secondary Commission carefully investigated the situation and then permitted the three affected high schools to resign their memberships on the plea that their being closed prevented their meeting NCA requirements on length of term. Although nothing in the public announcements from the Commission indicated anything other than that the resignation had been entirely voluntary, it appears to have been well understood that the alternative to resignation was being dropped by action of the Association. When the schools reopened in 1959-1960—desegregated —they had to apply for accreditation on the same terms required for new schools. The Commission did not then nor later issue a firm policy statement defining its position in regard to continuing accreditation of member schools that refused to integrate in defiance of the law. However, it did take steps to indicate that it would not consider for accreditation schools opened in order to evade the ruling of the Supreme Court.

A related problem, because it usually involved minorities, was the increasing difficulties of the inner-city high school. Diminishing financial support, overcrowding, and the flight of teachers along with their white constituencies to the suburbs raised questions, usually about standards, which directly concerned the Association. The urban high school was, for example, a major item for discussion at the Commission's fall meeting in 1962; an informal committee was formed to consider their special problems, and some flexibility was introduced in the application of criteria to such schools. A not uncommon charge raised in the multischool city districts was that the racially imbalanced ghetto schools were being discriminated against financially and in other ways. A statement in the criteria for high schools clearly forbade such practices: "membership in the Association shall not be maintained when it is evident that this is being done at the expense of the [other] schools in the district." Although progress of a sort, this was clearly less than the firm leadership for urban schools that some of the Association's own leaders called for and which the times demanded.

A good deal of innovation, in a sense, consisted of carrying forward and refining old policies, themselves innovations of another era. The activities issue, for one, that had been so alive in the years immediately after the war, had been brought to the status of an arrangement that was reasonably satisfactory all around. The National Association of Secondary School Principals' list of approved contests and activities was approved by the Commission in 1962, and a revised statement of policies and guidelines was published a year later. Both moves were attempts to rationalize the control of extra-curricular activities in order to prevent any possibility of their becoming the private province of the coaches, associations, and local enthusiasts.

In some measures the changes in Commission procedures and policies followed or coincided with what the Higher Commission was doing. The status of provisional membership set up for high schools in 1966 for schools preparing to apply for accreditation had some similarities to practices earlier established by the Higher Commission. A training program begun two years later for chairmen of examining committees had its counterpart in the Higher Commission's consultant-examiner training program.

The Secondary Commission was also moving toward easing some of the once strict requirements for teacher preparation, especially for teachers of highly technical-vocational subjects. The development of a vast new area of occupational education also came under consideration by FRACHE. In 1967 FRACHE proposed the creation of a National Committee for Occupational Education to promote the development and improvement of vocational education and to disseminate information about good occupational programs already in operation.[9]

Yet the vehement advocates of articulation in the secondary schools and in their Commission seem somehow to have overlooked the significance to their cause in the movements noted above and the shared concern about vocational education.[10] Although insufficient cooperation between the accrediting commissions and the lack of coordination of their goals and operations remained matters of much concern, the developments in educational methods and outlook in the schools and colleges were promoting coordination; that is, it was being achieved from the operational level, and accreditation was in a sense a device to sanction and institutionalize what was going on.

In their proceedings and dealing with their constituencies, however, the two accrediting commissions continued to be rather markedly different. At the annual Association meeting, for example, the Committees by Type of the College Commission held hearings on college accreditation applications somewhat in the manner of a Congressional committee, with the representatives of applicant institutions appearing formally before the committees to state their case and to answer questions. Having no such committees, the Secondary Commission customarily held no formal

---

9. FRACHE, Mimeographed statement, October 1967.

10. Lowell Fisher, "An Analysis of Problems of Articulation and Suggestions for Action," *NCAQ*, XXXV (July 1960), pp. 11-16; Summary of joint meeting, June 18, 1964, of NCA Board of Directors, Executive Bodies of the Commissions, Chairman of Committee on Publications and Information Service, and Retiring Chairman of Long-Range Planning Committee.

hearings at the annual meeting, although on occasion representatives of institutions were given the opportunity to present a case for themselves in response to a commission ruling. For the most part, however, the time was spent in examining high schools' annual reports. Principals and superintendents were assembled at the annual Association meeting to read the reports and point out any possible deviation from criteria. Working in a large meeting room in the Palmer House in Chicago, where annual meetings were held for many years, they assembled in groups by states, separated from other groups by curtain partitions. Here, sitting around large tables and under the supervision of members of the Commission, examiners worked in groups of two or three reading reports of high schools from states other than their own. Enough reviewers—six or seven hundred—were brought in from member high schools each year to complete the work in a single day. The procedure, intended as a guarantee of impartiality, provided a considerable measure of participatory democracy and a practical orientation in the workings of the Association as well.

Some hints of the need for committees by type to evaluate high schools were appearing in the contradictions and inconsistencies involved in judging small rural high schools, inner-city ghetto schools, and advanced suburban institutions by a single set of standards. The reemphasis upon individuality and relevance to the ideals of a teaching staff or the needs of a community and a body of students that were so much a part of the 1967-1968 Policies and Criteria pointed the way to a multi-standard similar to that developed for colleges and universities.

Indeed, a separate procedure for a distinct type of institution was introduced in 1968 when the Commission began accrediting junior high schools. (The Southern Association had begun accrediting them in 1954.)[11] Discussion of the advisability of this move had begun in the early 1950's, but it was not until the end of the decade that the first concrete steps toward accrediting was

11. Ellsworth Sheldon Statler, "Recent Growth Patterns of Accreditation of Secondary Schools by the Regional Accrediting Associations," *National Association of Secondary School Principals Bulletin*, XLV (October 1961), pp. 16-22.

taken, and then it was nearly another decade before accreditation was actually begun. Among the reasons for the long delay was the reluctance to add more work for an already overburdened Commisssion at the almost certain cost of leaving little time for the Commission to provide any sort of thoughtful leadership. Junior high school principals had some misgivings about the possible imposition of controls upon their schools by the high schools, although for the most part the principals seemed to favor an accreditation program, provided it were done carefully and with due regard for the sensibilities of all the parties concerned.

In 1959 following the receipt of a resolution from the Kansas Association of Secondary School Principals, the Commission appointed a subcommittee to survey the junior high schools to sound out their sentiment on the matter, to find out what ideas the junior high school people might have about standards and procedures, and to locate personnel who could assist in developing a program. About two-thirds of both junior and senior high school principals wanted to proceed.[12] The following spring another committee was appointed to investigate further the feasibility of developing junior high accrediting. On the basis of its recommendations, which were favorable, the Commission expanded the committee and charged it with the responsibility of formulating policies and procedures.[13]

Using the *Evaluation Guide for Junior High Schools* developed by the National Study of Secondary School Evaluation sponsored by the American Council on Education, the committee held an accreditation trial run on about seventy schools. It did not work particularly well. Some schools were weeks and even months in getting through their self-surveys. The National Study *Evaluation Guide* was criticized severely for being largely a copy of the high school *Guide*. The committee concluded that "there exists no satisfactory self-study instrument for self-evaluation of junior high

12. Stephen A. Romine, "Opinions about North Central Association Accreditation of Junior High Schools," *NCAQ*, XXXVI (Fall 1961), pp. 193-200.

13. Everett V. Samuelson, "The Accreditation of Junior High Schools by the North Central Association of Colleges and Secondary Schools," *NCAQ*, XXXVII (Winter 1963), pp. 233-236.

schools. . . ," and instructed the trial schools to use whatever guide was approved or devised by its state committee.

Meanwhile, a set of "Policies, Principles, and Standards for the Approval of Junior High Schools" was completed and referred to the state committees and junior high principals for their discussion and reaction. Following further revision, an accreditation procedure was formally approved by the Association in 1967. The final step before the first examining teams were sent out in the fall and winter of that year was to hold a brief training clinic for the thirty-five men and women who were to be chairmen of the first teams. Pending the accreditation of enough junior high schools to warrant a permanent structure, an interim associate state chairman for junior high schools was nominated by each state association of junior high principals and formally appointed by the Commission.

The standards for junior high school accreditation were divided into three levels for each of eight general principles. The "A" standards, structural and largely quantitative, were those "discernible by their physical presence." "B" standards, related to the operation and conduct of the program, were designed to "discriminate between good and bad practices," in short, were qualitative. "C" standards related to program improvement and continuous evaluation.

In 1968 the program was still too new for any proper assessment of its effects. Junior high schools had always been under supervision of their respective state departments of education, and they had always been under much influence from the high schools since they had to prepare their students for high school matriculation. Whether the new program would produce enough improvements to warrant the extra work it involved, only the future would determine. The junior high schools—i.e., their principals—wanted association accreditation; and if the publicity individual schools distributed after they had been accredited is any reliable measure, accreditation was worth a great deal to those schools that received it. Certainly no one could charge that the NCA had been actively seeking power over the junior high schools, or that it had been less than careful to give full consideration to all the parties concerned.

The junior high schools were the beneficiaries, not only of the long experience with high school accreditation, but also of the most recent developments in education, for the Commission was simultaneously developing a revision of its policies and criteria for high schools. Emphasis, as has been previously noted, was on experimentation, continuing improvement, and flexibility. Even the format of the two guides closely resembled each other. Each criterion for the high schools (nine in all) was introduced by a brief statement of "qualitative principles" followed by an extended outline of "minimum standards," and concluded with several brief statements on "exceptional or optimal conditions." The latter were guidelines of improvement for accredited institutions. Here the Commission attempted to specify just what was meant by self-improvement. Under Criterion III, "Institutional Program," were included the encouragement of diagnostic tests to determine the nature of student learning, opportunities in the fine arts "through arrangements other than performance courses in arts and music," measures to decrease students' dependence upon their teachers, and arrangements for cooperative and team teaching. Other goals included travel grants to teachers to attend professional meetings, and the employment of increasing numbers of para-professional personnel to relieve teachers of non-teaching duties. Of particular interest was the introduction of a Criterion on "Institutional Adaptability," prefaced by the following statement of principle:

> The school shall be so organized as to foster experimentation and innovation designed to adapt the institution effectively to changing conditions and objectives. Employing new approaches in curriculum, organization, and technology, the school shall attempt to develop effective practices which capitalize on the school's strengths and correct the school's weaknesses.

Schools were encouraged to devote a minimum of one percent of their operating budget for research and development.

In the little more than a decade since the mid-1950's the Commission had embarked on its most revolutionary and what might also prove to be its most influential course since it had begun accrediting high schools. It is to the credit of the Commission on Secondary Schools that, despite its long tradition of bringing high schools up to an ideal that was perhaps more static than changing —although less static than the college ideal—it was able to shift over to a search for a new "ideal" of excellence when the times called for it. The somewhat loosely organized high school Commission, close to the grass roots, was not only accepting change in secondary education but was seeking to shape it. For the most part the changes to which it was adjusting were in the nature of more exacting and more sophisticated standards for teachers, a reordering and an expansion of the curriculum, a reexamination of teaching methods with attention to the new technology of teaching, and a sharpened sense of the direct social responsibility of educational institutions and the education they provided.

VI

Improving Teacher Preparation and Curriculum: The Commission on Research and Service

Perhaps neither of the accrediting commissions was as conscious of the need for promoting constructive change in the schools and colleges as the Commission on Research and Service. At the same time, however, its role in the Association was never entirely clear and in some respects became even less so as the two accrediting commissions undertook with increasing frequency to set up their own research task forces to deal with the problems encountered. It also suffered from having no permanent staff. While both of the other commissions had permanent secretaries and salaried clerical personnel, the Commission on Research and Service continued to depend upon volunteer elected secretaries who changed regularly. It lacked machinery to give cohesiveness to its work or to see that its projects were brought to completion. In fact, it seems fair to say that the Commission hardly worked as a single organization at all, but instead as a loosely connected group of committees and subcommittees operating semi-independently of each other and with whatever energy and purpose they got from their own members.

A strong defender of the Commission's role in the Association has described its procedure thus:

. . . from some quarter there comes a suggestion that this or that problem is an important one, that it should be studied by a committee, and that the results of its findings should be reported. The Steering Committee recommends to the Board of Directors that the committee be established. A chairman is secured and he usually has much to do with the selection of the members. The committee meets, usually not more than two or three times a year and decides what it will do. Often one or more members develop a procedure for finding out what is being done on the matter by member schools, what the problems are, and possible steps which might be considered. Then the committee prepares a report, usually with suggestions or recommendations. The report is published in some form.

Committee activities are reported from time to time to the Steering Committee, to the Commission at its annual meeting, and to the Board. Many of the problems are of the kind that are seldom solved in any final way. Therefore, there is almost always more to be done, more information to be secured, and more recommendations to report. No terminal date was established for most committees. As long as committee interest continues, so does the work of the committee.

It is also important to note that the purpose of many committees has been to get some basic findings and recommendations into the main stream of thinking among member schools and, especially, among the readers of the *Quarterly* and those who attend the annual meetings. Therefore, a number of committees have pointed their effort toward articles or reports in the journal of the Association. Others have pointed their effort toward presentations at the annual meeting. For many years almost all of the small group sessions at the annual meetings were opportunities for interested representatives to hear a report, to discuss it, and, hopefully, to carry away some helpful ideas. This, in a way, is both research and service. No directives are issued to member schools. If the work of the committee brings about change, it is due to the fact that educational leaders get some good ideas and relate them to their own institution and its program. It is likely that this procedure is quite proper, in full accordance with the purpose of the Commission as set forth in the by-laws and the results are of real value to member schools, even though one cannot point often to a particular committee report that may have, in itself, resulted in great change.

In short, the Commission operated essentially as a convenient pool of NCA personnel drawn together less for any specific duties than by virtue of their expertise and/or interest, and the willingness and leisure to think about any sort of educational problem. However much this unstructured quality might be valued inside the Commission, the situation periodically led to questions about its role. They arose chiefly because there was never complete agreement among the three NCA Commissions about the proper route for originating research services: whether they should be initiated by the Research and Service Commission and should be concerned with the "big issues," or whether they should originate in the workaday needs of the accreditation commissions and on their specific request. In December 1968, for example, the Executive Board of the Commission on Colleges and Universities approved a proposal outlining a program of research which that Commission would conduct itself.

Yet, the Commission on Research and Service made significant contributions to the progress of education and to the work of the Association. Its long-time interest in the art of teaching and its many inquiries into the problems of improving teaching on every level of education were substantial contributions. Some of its work with curriculum, most notably the Foreign Relations Project, produced a permanent and long-overdue change in the content of American social studies education. No less timely and positive were the Commission's programs concerned with the talented and with the culturally disadvantaged, and those concerned with easing the increasing social tensions surrounding the schools.

Improvement of teaching continued to be the central concern of the Commission in the last decade and a half of the Association's history, as it had been in fact since the Commission was first organized. The oldest, and one might say the most basic, program in this area was the Liberal Arts Project. Begun in 1941 to raise the quality of public school teachers by improving the liberal arts colleges so many of them attended, it had become an

NCA institution apparently destined to continue indefinitely, although participation had declined to thirty or so colleges by the end of the 1960's, about half the number of the peak years of a decade earlier.

The direct linkage between the program and the preparation of teachers had pretty much given way, however, to a more direct cooperative concern with the improvement of various aspects of the participating colleges themselves. It had become in a sense a cooperative improvement program for the less prestigious and more insecure liberal arts colleges in the NCA area, and for some a sort of accreditation preparatory program.[1] In its annual report of March 1968, the supervisory Subcommittee on Liberal Arts reported activities that had become more or less routine over the years: annual two- to four-week workshops in higher education, annual advisory visits by members of the coordinating staff to the participating colleges, and occasional regional conferences. (These had played a larger part in the early days of the Project than they did after 1960.)

A relatively new activity was the annual seminar for new college teachers begun in 1964. Originally financed by a Danforth Foundation grant, it was successful enough to continue on a self-supporting basis after the grant was exhausted—that is, it was financed by participating colleges. Twenty-three young teachers attended the first workshop. In 1967 forty-four participated in a summer workshop at Hope College to discuss general issues in higher education and to receive help in developing the new courses they would have to teach in their new jobs.[2] Yet, however meritorious and necessary such a program would appear to be, the number of participating young teachers was never more than a small percentage of those actually beginning their careers each year in the NCA area.

The companion program for teachers colleges, established in 1948, had become almost equally institutionalized. Although

1. Lewis B. Mayhew, "Report of the Committee on Liberal Arts Education," *NCAQ*, XXXII (April 1958), pp. 288-290.
2. John Hollenbach, "Seminar for New College Teachers," *NCAQ*, XXXIX (Spring 1965), pp. 318-321.

from the beginning it had never had nearly as many participating colleges as the parent program, its clientele remained more stable with as many colleges participating (between twenty and twenty-five) in 1968 as there had been when the program began. Services to the colleges included the monthly news bulletin and "packet service" shared with the Liberal Arts College Project, coordinator visits, and an annual workshop. In some contrast to the liberal arts college program, which had not only veered away from its original purpose but appeared to be running down, the teachers college subcommittee concentrated directly on the improvement of high school teacher education. As a rule it dealt with specific problems of teaching and not with such matters as orienting new college teachers or with the larger issues of the overall purpose of a college. Indeed, it was the most effective of the programs to improve teacher education in the colleges mainly because of its clear emphasis and the continuity and vigor of the subcommittee's leadership—only two men had chaired it to 1969.

The last teacher training group to be organized, the subcommittee for multi-purpose colleges, set up in 1950, never managed to work out a program which was satisfactory to the committee itself or interesting to the colleges of education on university campuses. The committee arranged several sessions at annual meetings of the Association, and in 1964 it completed a survey of graduate programs in education at multi-purpose institutions. In 1968 the committee, on its own request, was discharged by the Commission with not much to show for nearly twenty years of existence.

A more specific attack on the problem of improving teaching was envisioned in 1956 when, on the request of the Commission on Colleges and Universities, a Subcommittee on Student Teaching was formed. After considerable investigation as well as some indecision about the best course to follow, the subcommittee completed two surveys. The results of the first appeared under the title of "Some Guiding Principles for Student Teaching Programs."[3] The second was reported in a mimeographed thirty-five

3. *NCAQ*, XXXII (October, 1957), pp. 193-196.

page summary entitled "Student Teaching in Schools of the North Central Association Area." The report was distributed to the directors of teacher training in NCA colleges.[4]

Two other problems that the subcommittee set out to investigate were the impact of student teachers (1965) and teaching interns (1967) upon the quality of the schools in which they practiced and the possible effects upon standards and accreditation. The Commission on Secondary Schools, faced with the problem of evaluating the high school programs, was becoming apprehensive about the development of such programs without much guidance from anyone in the Association, and their possible exploitation by schools looking for a way to get inexpensive teachers. A survey made in 1967-1968 indicated that the practice was not only widespread but that it had no real format or standards. The committee recommended that evaluation teams inquire into the use of such programs and advise the Secondary Commission to develop guidelines for internships in the NCA.[5]

Improving teaching on the job, another long-standing concern of the Commission, continued to be the subject of a variety of projects and reports, most, although not all of them, the work of the In-Service Education for Teachers Subcommittee. Five formal studies and a number of other projects in the secondary field were completed by 1960. One of the most useful programs as well as the most promising in the long run for the improvement of high school courses and articulation of college and high school education was the promotion of subject-matter conferences of high school and college teachers. "Pilot workshops" in English and science were organized in 1961, and full conferences were held or planned for each NCA state in 1963-64.[6]

The need for similar attention to the colleges had been partly supplied at least by the Liberal Arts Project and the teacher edu-

4. A capsule version was published in *NCAQ*, XXVII (Winter, 1963), pp. 237-250.

5. Prudence B. Dyer, "Teacher Internship Programs in NCA Institutions," *NCAQ*, XLIII (Fall 1968), pp. 213-223.

6. "Two Conferences for College-High School Subject Matter Teachers," *NCAQ*, XXXVII (Fall 1962), pp. 191-207.

cation program. But by the late 1950's booming college enrollments and the inevitable accompanying faculty shortages, which would only result in the employment of increasing numbers of inexperienced and partially trained people, opened a new field of action. Upon the initiative of the Association for Higher Education's Committee on Teaching, the Commission on Research and Service joined with the AHE to hold a national round table on college teaching in 1961 in Chicago. A College Teacher Project was considered for a time but about all that came of it was a new Subcommittee on Research and Service.[7]

Commission activities in the area of teaching also included improvement of the curriculum and the effective use of machines or communications media. As has been noted earlier, the Association's efforts to shape curricular content directly by developing new courses and study guides in a variety of areas had been only marginally successful at best until the development of the Foreign Relations Project. This program, launched at a crucial time and with generous financial support and expert staffing, would practically monopolize the role of the semi-moribund Committee on Experimental Units, and eventually would be included in the committee's name.

In its first years of operation, in addition to its highly successful publication program, the Project sponsored several hundred one- or two-day conferences for teachers; it later shifted to sponsoring state-wide "residential" seminars and conferences on specific areas or issues of foreign policy, among them the Ohio State University Conference on India in April 1959 and the Michigan State University Conference on Africa in June of the same year.[8]

The Project staff also spent a considerable proportion of its time visiting schools and workshops, and in disseminating information it gathered about foreign relations teaching and trends in

7. Richard H. Davis, "College Teacher Project—a Summary Report," *NCAQ*, XXXVII (Winter 1963), pp. 251-254.

8. James M. Becker, "The NCA Foreign Relations Project," *Social Education*, XXIII (October 1959), pp. 274-276, 296; Becker, "Education for Participation in World Affairs," *National Association of Secondary School Principals' Bulletin*, XLIV (October 1960), pp. 143-150. Becker was the first director of the Project.

the social studies generally. By 1960 over 3,500 schools were participating in the Project and using the eight pamphlets it had published (thirty-two high schools had been in the pilot program four years before). A total of $40,000 was realized from the sale of booklets in 1959-1960, with a total of 60,000 booklets distributed by the end of the year.[9] In 1961, Laidlaw Brothers, a commercial publisher, undertook to publish and sell the booklets. On the occasion of its tenth anniversary in 1965, the project published its eleventh booklet, Robert Scalapino's *Japan: Ally in the Far East,* and total sales of booklets for the year came to nearly 150,000, almost treble the number of only five years before.

Although no further major foundation support was forthcoming, the Project received some smaller grants from such sources as the Harris Foundation ($20,000 in 1961) and the Asia Foundation ($6,000 in 1962), and an incalculable amount of assistance, including some cash, from such organizations as the African-American Institute, the American Assembly, the American Association for the United Nations, the Asia Society, the American Political Science Association, the American Jewish Committee, the Foreign Policy Association, and a dozen or so others.

To some enthusiasts at least, the time seemed at hand for a major effort to reform the high school social studies curriculum. The Project report of 1961 summarized major trends in the high schools under the title of *Points of Take-off in the Social Studies.* A year later the Association formed an *ad hoc* subcommittee on the social sciences and authorized the Foreign Relations Project to survey the status of the social studies programs in the schools. The general conclusion of the report—one might suggest that it was also its inspiration—was that the social studies were in a state of flux and that the time had come to develop a "single, compact program similar to those developed for the natural sciences. . . ."[10] The director of the Project reported also that nearly

9. "A Report on the NCA Foreign Relations Project, February 1955—September 1961," Chicago, September 28, 1961.
10. "NCA's Role in the Social Studies," *NCAQ,* XXXVIII (Fall 1963), pp. 163-165.

forty experimental social studies programs were already in operation in the NCA region under the sponsorship of universities, book publishers, and foundations.[11] A standard complaint about high school social science programs before the modifications induced by the Foreign Relations Project and various other demands for changes in the late 1950's was that they had remained substantially unaltered since 1916.

Supporters of the proposal urged that the NCA assume leadership of this movement by sponsoring paid teams of high school teachers and university professors to experiment with and to develop new social studies programs. Hopefully to be financed with one to three million dollars to be secured from foundations, the "consultant program," as it came to be called, was brought forward by the Committee on Experimental Units and the newly created Subcommittee on the Social Sciences and presented to the Commisssion on Secondary Schools in 1966. There it failed to win approval and the Committee on Social Science was dissolved on the request of its chairman.

It was not a total setback, however, for the Foreign Relations Project continued to serve as a consultative body on social studies programs, and numerous experiments or innovations in the general area continued to enjoy a quasi-sponsorship by the Association. In 1968 the supervisory Committee on Experimental Units reported five residential seminars during the preceding year, numerous in-service and pre-service demonstrations of innovative social science teaching strategies, participation in the programs of such professional societies as the American Political Science Association and the International Studies Association, the revision of five of its Foreign Relations Series booklets, the preparation of two new ones, circulation of reports of seminars and conferences. Other activities included cooperation with United States Aid to Education Title III programs, the Illinois Curriculum Council, and the National Center of School and College Television.

11. James M. Becker, "The Dynamics of Change," *NCAQ*, XXXIX (Winter 1963), p. 275.

On August 31, 1969, unable to obtain sufficient funds for the ongoing program and newly proposed activities, the NCA Foreign Relations Project was terminated. The Project had not ended, however. On the contrary, it had achieved what the NCA hoped for when it launched any experimental program. High school curricula had been significantly and permanently affected, and the Project had won independent sponsorship; an independent publisher, Laidlaw Brothers, had assumed responsibility for printing and distributing the eleven-booklet *Foreign Relations Series* some years before; and many of the Project's activities had been adopted by the School Services Division of the Foreign Policy Association, headed since 1966 by the first director of the NCA Project.

Such internal issues as may have affected the decision to discontinue the ambitious plan for reforming the social science curriculum are not revealed in the Association or Commission minutes, but in part at least the decision was in response to a growing concern among some Association leaders that the NCA was weakening its central role—accreditation—by undertaking activites beyond its capacity to manage or to finance them and at the cost of draining off the funds and personnel it had to use for its central function. In effect, a sort of informal understanding was developing that the Association would sponsor large projects only if funds could be obtained from some source other than dues and fees. Moreover, there was a growing disposition among some Association members to leave experimentation to the private organizations, and especially to the universities. On the other hand, the Project had demonstrated that the Association could indeed directly affect curriculum if it brought enough money, energy, and organization to bear.

The developing role of technological devices in teaching was another issue of the postwar era that continued to engage the Commission through its Subcommittee on Television, dating back to 1953, and a new Subcommittee on the Instructional Use of the Electronic Computer, formed in 1967. The older committee could claim a considerable role in taming the "medium" to academic uses. When the committee was first formed, television had already made its debut on the NCA educational scene. The initial task had then been to find out what was already being done. The next step was to secure data on the costs and possible uses as well as the limitations of television in a modern instructional situation of huge enrollments, rising costs, and persistent teacher shortages. In 1958 a demonstration of educational television was arranged for the annual meeting of the NCA in Chicago, and the *Quarterly* published a symposium (its second report—the first appeared in 1954) entitled "An Appraisal of the Current Status of Television as a Medium of Instruction."[12]

With this for a beginning, the subcommittee set out to secure support for a thorough study. The United States Office of Education supplied funds for a series of conferences and for publications. In 1959 an initial grant of $20,000 financed a seminar of NCA leaders and TV experts and the publication of its subsequent report (1961), *The Uses of Television in Education*.[13] It advised small institutions to consider supplementing their curricula by TV instruction from other institutions, suggested that large institutions consider TV as a device to improve their teaching effectiveness, and urged the teacher training institutions to orient their prospective teachers in TV use. Faculties in general were encouraged to engage in cooperative in-service studies of the medium. The Office of Education and national educational organizations were also called upon to study the uses of TV.

In the next several years the subcommittee received regular subventions from Federal funds to finance a series of conferences and seminars. A pilot conference on "Principles and Practices in the Use of Television in Education" at Ohio State University in November 1960, brought together representatives from every NCA state and from the other regional accrediting associations.[14] The next year the subcommittee arranged five state and three regional TV conferences involving teachers, legislators, and admin-

12. *NCAQ,* XXXII (April 1958), pp. 357-367.
13. When availability of the report was announced in several educational journals, more than 5,000 requests came from every state of the union and several foreign countries.
14. *NCAQ,* XXXV (October 1960), p. 293.

istrators of the Association area. Planning meetings and "depth seminars" were also held in 1963 and 1964 with financial assistance from the United States Office of Education. One immediate effect of these conferences was to stimulate other regional groups such as the Southern Regional Education Board to hold conferences of their own.

It would be difficult to overestimate the importance of the subcommittee's work. When expectations and speculation (combined with misinformation and false leads) might easily have led to serious and costly, even harmful, applications of the television medium, the Commission on Research and Service had taken vigorous action to study the subject and to establish rational, deliberate approaches to developing guidelines. Educational bodies were stimulated to reserve UHF stations as they became available, to form Education-TV station networks, and to develop joint TV tape libraries. Moreover, the pattern of cooperation between the Association and the United States Office of Education added one more precedent for the development of a working combination of regional-institutional independence and Federal assistance.

The computer subcommittee filed its first formal report at the annual NCA meeting of 1968. At its first meeting, in the preceding November, the committee had taken some steps toward gathering information on educational uses of the computer preparatory to circulating the latest and most reliable information to NCA schools, and as preparation for developing policies and guidelines for the schools. It seems quite probable that with this matter, as with educational TV, the Association was in a strong position to guide its membership through the maze of claims—many of them exaggerated and/or self-serving—to a knowledgeable incorporation of another sophisticated technology into the teaching and management of schools and colleges.

Another group of problems to which the Commission addressed itself arose from the social and community tensions that would become the central preoccupation of Americans in the

1960's, even to the extent of effecting a decline of attention to the foreign relations issues that seemed so central immediately after World War II. The first glimmer of official Association concern was the *Quarterly's* publication in October 1945 of an article entitled "The Study of Inter-group Relations," which observed almost casually that "one notes a marked unrest among so-called 'minority peoples' in every part of the nation."

It was another decade, however, before the NCA took official action to deal with a worsening situation. In 1956 the Commission on Research and Service recommended an "exploratory committee" on human relations; a committee was fully established in 1957, and some months later given a budget of $3,200 from Association funds and a supplemental grant from B'nai B'rith to finance its initial investigations. In its first meeting the new subcommittee proposed three studies: (1) a bibliography of relevant studies, (2) a survey of current practices in teacher education that might be useful for pre-service teachers, and (3) a survey of recently graduated teachers' opinions on what they should have been taught about human relations problems. During the next three years the committee published the results of its studies in the *Quarterly*: "Teacher Education for Human Relations in the Classroom"; "Human Relations in the Classroom: A Study of Problems and Situations Reported by 1075 Second-Year Secondary School Teachers"; and "Human Relations in the Classroom: A Challenge to Teacher Education."[15]

The first of these, based on the results of a faculty survey (1108 professors from 336 colleges responded to a questionnaire), revealed that the majority of college teachers felt there was a need for specific training and that most also believed that they themselves were doing something to broaden perspectives and induce tolerance, especially with reference to inter-racial feelings. Only a minority, however, felt any real personal responsibility for such teaching or thought that it should have a major

15. *NCAQ*, XXXVI (Winter 1962), pp. 278-291; XXXVII (Winter 1963), pp. 260-279; XXXVIII (Winter 1964), pp. 257-270.

role in the specific subjects they taught. In the words of the report, "the direct learning experiences which are most effective in changing attitudes, in developing sensitivity, and establishing values and skills were used by only a small percentage of the respondents."

It was even more evident in the responses of the 1072 second-year secondary school teachers in the Association schools who completed the subcommittee's questionnaire that teacher preparation programs in the colleges did little in any specific way to equip them to deal with the tense situations they were going to encounter in the schools. The replies ranged from expressions of bewildered concern from the more sensitive to indications of the most callous inability to understand the frustrations of people disadvantaged by race, by religious diverseness, or by cultural and economic poverty. Indeed, a startling number of these young teachers indicated by their answers that they were actually not aware of the existence of the problems about which they were being questioned. Their answers indicated too that their family or community or church background contributed more to their effective management of decent human relations among their pupils than any formal training they had received when they were studying to be teachers. College courses were, however, considered by these teachers to be of considerable value in preparing them to deal with students of widely ranging abilities.

In view of the findings, it is a matter of no surprise that the subcommittee devoted itself, not to offering advice to the colleges and young teachers on how and what to teach and study in order to promote good human relations, but to describing in detail just what such relations were. That is, the first step to be taken was to convince the colleges and their students that human relations problems existed and deserved attention. In trying to deal with nothing less than the reformation of human attitudes, it was exceedingly difficult even to arrive at a firm position from which to advise the teacher-training institutions or their graduates. And the subcommittee essentially settled for calling attention to the various manifestations of the problem and advising the schools to set up in-service programs for their teachers.

In time, however, several programs were developed to cope with specific aspects of the tensions and deprivations that would come under the rubric of human relations. One of the most prominent was the improvement of the schools' response to the widely varying abilities of their students. Concern over the neglect of talent had first been strongly expressed during the war, when manpower and talent shortages were suddenly pressing issues, and was reinforced in the years immediately after by the military, moral, and economic competition of the Cold War, and by the sudden dramatic entry of the Russians into space exploration. Vehement critics of "education" like Arthur Bestor and Hyman Rickover gained a wide hearing and considerable support in the press and certain academic circles for their charges that the schools offered little challenge to the intellectually gifted. In contrast to the rigorous and highly selective secondary schools of Europe, it seemed to such critics that American schools neglected the academically talented almost by design. The consequent failure to make the most of this human potential resulted in great social and economic loss to the country, to say nothing of its cost to the individual. In addition, students of economic development in the 1950's reinforced the rising concern by revising upward their estimates of the importance of the role of "human resources" as compared to the role of "natural resources" in the rate of economic growth.

One writer asserted that the American loss of talent was truly alarming, with fewer than half of the upper 25 percent of all high school graduates entering colleges, and fewer than 60 percent of the top 5 percent doing so. A manpower survey commission of the National Education Association asserted that each year a half million people able to graduate from college were not doing so, that in fact more than half of this group did not even begin. In the schools themselves, another writer pointed out, more than half the children with an I.Q. above 135 were unnecessarily held back in their age level grade in school because there was no means or willingness to locate them and accelerate their work.[16] Finally, a disproportionate share of the bright school dropouts came from disadvantaged racial and ethnic groups or from isolated rural areas.

Two years before Sputnik sailed across the heavens, the Executive Committee of the Association, on the advice of the Commission on Research and Service, appointed a Subcommittee for the Guidance and Motivation of Superior and Talented Students. In the next half dozen years it would develop into one of the most widely influential forces for change in education that the NCA had ever produced.

As was usually the case of every other successful NCA effort of this sort, this program had the benefit of a vigorous and resourceful committee chairman and an equally effective and experienced project director. It also received the adequate financing that such successful programs require to maintain a professional staff and to underwrite activities and publications: more than a quarter of a million dollars from the Carnegie Foundation (two major grants in 1958 and 1960), plus nearly $100,000 from the United States Office of Education to underwrite a guidance and counseling institute in 1959. The project benefitted enormously also from the nearly perfect timing of appearing on the scene when public support was enthusiastic and the schools were in desperate need of advice.

Much planning by the subcommittee had already gone into the project when the Commission on Research and Service announced receipt of the initial Carnegie grant to finance a two-year study. Its purpose was "to find, develop, and implement procedures and programs in secondary schools to identify, guide, and motivate superior and talented students in all fields of learning

16. *An Interim Report on the NCA-STS Project,* NCA, November 1959. Cited in the report: Dale Wolfle, *America's Resources of Specialized Talent* (New York: Harper and Bros., 1954); Norman Cutts and Nicholas Moseley, *Teaching the Bright and Gifted* (Englewood Cliffs: Prentice-Hall, 1957); L. M. Terman and Melita Oden, *The Gifted Child Grows Up* (Stanford: Stanford Univ. Press, 1947).

who would contemplate 'a thorough college education.' "[17] Subsequently popularly and officially known as the NCA Project for Superior and Talented Students (STS), it defined the STS themselves as those ranking in the upper 25 percent on national norms in tests of mental ability and/or achievement, or those who had comparable ability on the basis of other agreed-upon criteria.

One hundred high schools in the NCA area were selected as the basis of the first-stage study (615 of the 3,378 NCA high schools applied). Schools selected had to have a minimal enrollment of three hundred students, a college matriculation rate of fewer than 35 percent of their graduates, and fewer than 80 percent of their high-ability graduates matriculating. The program achieved national significance when other regional associations joined in, either as participants or as observers at planning conferences. Both the Southern and the New England Associations began conducting their own workshops in 1960.

Although the professional staff was disbanded in August 1961 with the expiration of the second Carnegie grant, the STS subcommittee continued to serve as a clearinghouse of ideas and a source of encouragement to schools in the NCA, and as the NCA representative to work with the Liaison Committee of the cooperating regional associations.[18] A number of publications on the subject of identifying and teaching superior students was sponsored or encouraged by the subcommittee; by 1969 no fewer than fifteen were available.

The effect of the STS project had been immediate in the schools. Its impact was felt far beyond the limits of the NCA. On the invitation of the Association, all of the other regional associations had participated from the beginning. In the Southern Association, for example, the school administration of Memphis went to extraordinary lengths to mobilize community support for a system-wide STS project.[19] By the end of the 1960's it was an un-

17. *NCAQ*, XXXII (April 1958), pp. 286-287.
18. Fact Sheet on STS Project, Mimeographed, September 1, 1961; *NCAQ*, XXXVI (Fall 1961), pp. 163-165.
19. D. Shelby Counce, *The Memphis Story* (Chicago: North Central Association, 1965).

progressive school indeed that did not at least give lip service to the doctrine that special efforts had to be made to locate and to encourage the exceptionally able student and that special measures were needed to teach him. In a general way most educators had always known this, but the Project provided a sense of urgency and with it the detailed advice and assistance necessary to involve busy teachers and harried administrators.

A significant, and not altogether expected, by-product of the project was the opening it afforded for such concrete measures in articulating high school and college curricula as giving college credit (advanced placement) courses for superior students. This move toward relaxing the sharp boundaries between high schools and colleges would in time lead to others like the increased willingness in college circles to waive all college requirements if they had already been met.

The corollary to this program of giving practical implementation to the long-held doctrine of adjusting teaching to students' individual differences was almost certain to follow, particularly in an age of increasing sensitivity about the "other America," the hitherto neglected elements in American society. Reporting in 1968, when it could view with considerable satisfaction a job well done for the Superior and Talented Students, the STS subcommittee observed that "the thrust has moved from the gifted child crusade to the current emphasis on social rights and the disadvantaged students."

To be sure, the Association had earlier sponsored programs that related directly to the problems of the disadvantaged. An example was the work of the Subcommittee on the Improvement of Reading in Colleges and Secondary Schools formed in 1954. Its chief accomplishment was the compilation of a report (1956) entitled "Improved Instruction in Reading," which was widely circulated in the Association. A survey of what was being done in the Association produced the interesting information that the colleges appeared to be more concerned about reading difficulties than the high schools. Most of the remedial work being done was by English departments, although most English teachers had no more training in techniques than teachers of any other subject. In the next decade, however, a considerable amount of expertise developed on the subject of reading, and extensive, sophisticated reading improvement programs became one of the marks of a good secondary school.[20]

A related problem which called forth another subcommittee was the education of the non-academic student. An appropriate report, "Better Education for Non-Academic Youth," was published in April 1957. It attempted to offer advice on how to deal with a problem that was the inevitable result of compulsory education, and which teachers had come to view as one of the crosses borne by a martyr profession. These students had for years either quietly suffered through an education that meant little to them, or had resorted to incorrigibility or rebellion, according to their temperaments. At best, they enjoyed only a partial visibility. Far too many of the teaching profession perforce regarded them as congenitally uneducable. But the awakening to the joys and opportunities of teaching the STS had also been a reminder of the existence of a reverse problem at the other end of every school's intellectual scale. With the sharpened consciousness came also the beginning of some understanding of the extremely complex factors underlying academic ambition and ability or the seeming lack of them.

"The Other America" in the schools was the subject of two major addresses at the NCA annual meeting in 1966,[21] and the Commission on Research and Service responded with an *ad hoc* committee to consider the role accrediting associations might play in reaching this group. The committee became a regular subcommittee of the Commission during the following year.

In 1969, a new project on Students with College Aptitude from Disadvantaged Environments (SCADE) was begun by the

20. Leonard Courtney, "Characteristics of a Good High School Reading Program," *NCAQ*, XLI (Fall 1966), pp. 204-212.

21. Samuel Brownell, "Preparing Teachers for the Disadvantaged," *NCAQ*, XLI (Winter 1967), pp. 249-253; George W. Denemark, "Off-Campus Involvement of Students in the Education of the Disadvantaged," *Ibid.*, pp. 263-270.

STS Project Committee. Following the compilation of replies to an inquiry addressed to about two hundred NCA schools and colleges (about half replied), a conference of representatives of the responding institutions was held in Chicago immediately preceding the annual meeting of the Association. A report and recommendations were discussed further in an open conference session at the meeting. At this writing, the committee is considering a publication covering the initial survey, the reports from member institutions, and information gleaned from the 1969 annual meeting workshop. The committee is also planning another one day or one and a half day workshop at the 1970 annual meeting. Although SCADE was in a sense the counterpart of STS, it should be noted that the NCA had avoided the pitfall of open university admissions for minority groups into which some institutions, even some of the most prestigious, were in some danger of falling, by carefully limiting its concern to "students with *college* aptitudes."

In all the programs to create an educational approach and an education that had some value for the "atypical" members of the school population, the formulation of effective techniques to guide and motivate such students invariably occupied a central position. Of course, the idea that schools should give proper attention to student counseling was nothing new in educational circles. The first NCA Subcommittee on Guidance was appointed in 1947. Its studies, reported in three articles published in the *Quarterly*,[22] had provided the basis for the Secondary Commission's accreditation standards on guidance programs in the 1950's. Having completed its work, the first subcommittee dissolved, but in only a short time the entire issue of counseling was raised again, this time with special reference to the non-normal student.

Accordingly, a new subcommittee was formed in 1958 to explore the need for a thorough restudy of what actually was being done about counseling in NCA high schools. A full report of findings gathered from a survey of one hundred representative high schools was published in 1962. The study deliberately aimed

22. October 1947, January 1949, and October 1949.

at drawing attention to and implementing the Secondary Commission's new (1960) progress criteria on guidance-counselor personnel, the modest goal of one qualified counselor per three hundred students.[23]

In the eleven small high schools studied, although their counselor-student ratio was within the prescribed standard, most programs were in the initial stages of development. Medium-sized schools (the twenty-one schools studied had an average of 680 students) had one full-time counselor and two part-time. As might be expected, the large high schools (averaging nearly 1500 students) had the better established and the more sophisticated programs and the better trained personnel, although their pupil-counselor ratio was above the recommended NCA minimum. Typical procedures reported by the schools were the customary ones associated with career or college orientation. The special problems associated with counseling the students of outstanding talent or those suffering from social and environmental deprivation were not mentioned in the report.

It was not until five years later that the Subcommittee on Guidance and Counseling reported the results of another study attempting to identify promising practices of school guidance programs for "problem" students.[24] Among a number of examples cited, the Pupil Personnel Bureau of the Chicago public schools was considered especially effective.

As significant as the altered focus of the new approach to counseling was the fact that guidance and classroom teaching were frequently being merged in a joint enterprise. The broadened conception of counseling was incorporated into the 1968 revision of Policies and Criteria for Secondary Schools. Although the recommended pupil-counselor ratio remained unchanged from what it had been a half dozen years before, the new criteria

23. Robert L. Gibson, "An Overview of Guidance in the Secondary Schools in the North Central Association," *NCAQ*, XXXVI (Winter 1962), pp. 253-263.

24. "Guidance Programs for Meeting the Challenge of Society's Needs," *NCAQ*, XLI (Winter 1967), pp. 263-270.

suggested incorporating teachers and supporting personnel into the programs, required special instruction and services to meet the needs of exceptional children, and advised that the services of a certified school psychologist be made available for helping students with learning and social-emotional problems.

Although this advice was specifically directed to the high schools, as indeed most of the efforts to deal with problems of individual differences had been, it had increasing applicability for the colleges—even those with the highest academic standards—as they began to establish programs for culturally deprived minority students. Admitting such students meant that even the most selective colleges were being subjected increasingly to the pressures and maladjustments arising from a wide range of intellectual abilities, emotional instabilities, and social origins among their student bodies.

The tendency away from elitism to social cross section in the colleges was a strong force for improving the articulation of high school and college education. Yet large areas of the two systems of education remained almost as separate entities, a situation which continued to concern the Commission on Research and Service. Its efforts to promote articulation in one way or the other had a fairly long history. It will be recalled that a Committee on High School-College Relationships had been formed in 1950. Its main accomplishment was a forty-six page progress report. Four years later, a Subcommittee on High School-College Articulation was created by the Research Commission. In its first report to the Association in 1954, the subcommittee promised an active program, expressed much optimism about its expectations for success, and announced its first study, the "Identification and Assessment of the Competencies Needed by Students for Success in College."

A substantial part of the committee's work consisted of identifying just what the problems were, both in the view of high school and college spokesmen, and selecting those that appeared to have some promise of being remedied. In May 1959 the committee asked 63 high schools and 54 colleges to judge the importance of ten areas for NCA action regarding closer high school-college articulation. The answers were tabulated in the January, 1960 *Quarterly*. The Association decision to make articulation the central theme of the 1960 annual meeting emphasized its urgency. At the April 1, 1960 general session of the NCA annual meeting, the chairman of the Secondary Commission Articulation Committee presented a summary of the many presentations and discussions on "Improving School-College Articulation"— the annual meeting theme.

In large part the issue took the form of the high schools' grievances against the colleges and *vice versa*. High school representatives complained about (1) the multiplicity of tests to which college-bound high school students were subjected in order to win scholarships or to be admitted to college; (2) the variation and multiplicity of admissions forms; (3) the irrelevance of many colleges' admissions requirements to their own "dominant character"; (4) the failure of colleges to devise admissions procedures to identify student characteristics indicative of probable failure or success in adjusting to a college environment; (5) the failure of colleges to make any real use in their own advisement programs of the massive data they demanded from high school advisers and principals; (6) college pressures on high schools to modify their curricula from the ideal of comprehensiveness in the direction of direct college preparation; and (7) perhaps the most fundamental of all, the colleges' indifference to the entire problem of articulation.

From the other side, a good many of the colleges' grievances were in the nature of criticisms of fundamental secondary school philosophy and standards. High schoools were said to be too lax academically to prepare students for college, and unable even to teach students how to study, to budget their time, or to assume personal responsibility. The result was that colleges had to set up elaborate personnel departments to nurse along the unprepared students they received. Other complaints from the colleges were that many high schools' curricula included too many frills, that high schools were reluctant to cooperate with colleges in planning sequential levels of work in certain fields—history and math for example—from high school into college, and that the schools generally did a poor job in identifying aptitudes for college education and motivating their students to go to college.[25]

An immediate effect of the attention drawn to the problem by the discussion at the annual meeting in 1960 was the Executive Committee's instruction to the Articulation Subcommittee to initiate an exhaustive study of the proliferation of external testing. Two reports of its findings were published in two special issues of *NCA Today*. Current and projected activities were announced in a *Quarterly* article (January 1961) and a second article, "Pros and Cons of External Testing Programs," appeared in the Fall 1961 issue.[26] The subcommittee maintained a lively interest in the possible implications for articulation arising from problems of poverty and other deprivations. Of some ironical interest, because it reflected the fact that high schools were becoming more experimental and flexible than the colleges, was the committee's concern for influencing students from "forward-looking" high schools into "tradition-bound" colleges. Another concern was the fact that a great many high school counselors appeared to be overly oriented to psychological counseling at the expense of educational guidance. It was undoubtedly a reflection of the committee chairman's own personal experience as a university director of admissions that the committee would maintain a continuing interest in establishing some sort of orderly procedures in the overwhelming amount of correspondence and application forms that accompanied college admissions practices.

A proposal to establish an effective operational approach in the form of a high school-college relations committee in each state was never realized, although moves toward articulation of curricula were somewhat more promising. In 1968, the NCA was

25. Lowell B. Fisher, "An Analysis of Problems of Articulation and Suggestions for Action," *NCAQ*, XXXV (July 1960), pp. 11-16. Fisher was chairman of a Committee on Relations with Colleges that had been set up by the secondary commission. In 1963, at Fisher's request, this committee was merged with a similar committee of the Commission on Research and Service.

26. Clyde Vroman, "First Report on Testing by External Agencies," *NCAQ*, XXXV (January 1961), pp. 223-225; Frank B. Womer, "Pros and Cons of External Testing Programs," *NCAQ*, XXXVI (Fall 1961), pp. 201-210.

considering a request from some of its subcommittees to sponsor a pilot project on articulation of high school-junior college programs. NCA activity also played a considerable role in stimulating the formation of a National Council on School-College Relations, which was formed in 1966. This group included representatives of the regional associations (the NCA committee affiliated with it in 1967), and national organizations of deans and counselors, collegiate registrars and admissions officers, junior colleges, secondary school principals, the Catholic Education Association, and others.[27]

The on-going nature of this problem and the continued effort to ease it had somewhat of the same perennially nagging quality as the issue of defining a firm role in the NCA for the Commission on Research and Service itself. Scarcely any experienced member of the Association would refuse to acknowledge the third commission's usefulness. And, as the preceding pages have shown, its contributions to the effectiveness of the Association and the cause of good education were substantial.

Yet, throughout the period of this history, questions continued to arise from time to time about the advisability of continuing the research services in a separate body or incorporating them into the accrediting commissions, particularly since these commissions not infrequently carried on research activities anyway. As it was, despite the co-equal rank of "commission" that the research body carried, it really lacked the main elements of equality: its budget was only a fraction of the accreditation budgets; and it had no on-going, year-to-year function. While the accrediting commissions enjoyed a great measure of autonomy and self-sufficiency, the Research and Service Commission was almost totally dependent on the other commissions. It was the one commission that could not stand alone.

The question of the Research Commission's status became more pointed when the Long-Range Planning Committee, formed in 1958, launched a general reexamination of the organization and

27. Minutes, National Council on School-College Relations, December 6-7, 1967.

function of the Association. A measure of the indecision about the Research Commission was that, although its budget was increased sufficiently in 1967 to provide for its first paid part-time secretary, final appointment to the position was postponed to await the outcome of further discussions to define the Commission's role, and presumably to decide whether it should achieve equal status with the other commissions, or whether it should be dissolved entirely. Inside the Commission, although there was a strong belief in its essential usefulness as a source of ideas and various useful studies, and particularly as a necessary bridge between the two accrediting commissions and the educational systems they represented, the question was considered to be grave enough in the fall of 1968 to call for an extended survey of its activities and its future role in the Association.

Recommendations of the Commission's Self-Evaluation Study were accepted by the NCA Board of Directors in July 1969. Henceforth, the membership of the Commission (twelve members chosen from the NCA high schools and twelve from the member colleges and universities, exclusive of the officers) was to be chosen directly by the two accrediting commissions. Members would serve for staggered three-year terms. Executive power was reposed in a Steering Committee consisting of a chairman, vice-chairman, and secretary (each chosen for two-year terms), and six others, three each from the high school and college membership. The reorganized Commission was charged with the responsibility to 1) "initiate, plan, and carry forward" research programs subject to the approval of the Association Board of Directors; 2) engage in such research or activity as the accrediting commissions might request; and 3) furnish leadership in interpreting research findings and focusing attention on problems in need of attention and study."[28]

The Board of Directors at its October 1969 meeting created a Committee on Research and Service Projects. This committee (comprised of six persons—two from each of the commissions—

28. Commission on Research and Service Self-Evaluation Report to the Board of Directors, June 29, 1969.

one representative from each of the commissions and the chairman must be a member of the Board of Directors) will be directly responsible to the Board of Directors, will review all proposals for research and service from all NCA bodies, and then make recommendations concerning the need and quality of each proposal.

For the most part the intention of the reorganization was to tie the Research Commission more closely than it had been to the accrediting bodies for effective investigation of immediate problems, and to enlarge its function to include far-flung independent investigations which could provide information and guidance for the future course of the Association. Moreover, enlarging the Commission's role to include investigations possibly leading to significant changes in NCA policies was a tacit admission that dealing with educational problems as they arose might no longer be adequate. In the increasingly charged atmosphere of the 1960's, which promised to become more intense in the next decade, it was becoming necessary to anticipate trends as well as to respond to them.

EPILOGUE

Twenty-Five Years On

The inevitable question that presents itself about the North Central Association, as for any self-appointed body, is whether it justifies its existence beyond the protection of its own vested interest. The answer to the question, and the conclusion of this historical survey, is that the NCA as an organization, and as an American educational leader in general, has been singularly devoted to promoting the interest of both society and individual, whatever exceptions there might appear on occasion in the form of selfish behavior or narrow vision.

One need only attend the annual public conventions of the Association or sit in its councils to affirm that helpfulness and concern about improving educational performance, as well as a large measure of understanding about why it often fails to meet expectations, are conspicuous in the Association's relations with the institutions which come under its scrutiny. Moreover, this spirit is one born of experience; the men who lead the NCA have been through the mill themselves; they understand the educational system as practitioners, not as bureaucrats or academic experts who supervise what they have never themselves been called upon to implement. At the same time, an almost painfully patient consideration has beneath it a firmness of purpose which can be and is called forth by evidence of wilfully shabby practice or persistently inadequate performance.

Good intentions notwithstanding, the final measure of worth for any organization as far as the public is concerned must be in terms of accomplishment. On this score, too, voluntary accrediting bodies have built a strong case. It is no exaggeration to say that the NCA and organizations like it managed to hold American high schools and colleges on a steady evolutionary course during one of the most critical periods—the quarter century after World War II. The educational system came through these trying times with little of the residue of internecine factionalism arising from exaggerated claims and charges that had accompanied the Progressive Education movement of a generation earlier. The overwhelming need for Federal assistance had been recognized and accommodated but without the centralization and bureaucratic controls that many had feared. Nor had the enormous expansion of activity, as well as of expenditures, been accompanied by declining educational standards—indeed, the quality of American education had actually been advanced.

Perhaps the most significant achievement of the regional accrediting associations was the encouragement of innovation and individuality in an era when centralization tendencies were powerful. In the post-war years high school education had been transformed—indeed revolutionized—by new technology, new subjects and techniques, and a new attention to social responsibilities. In the colleges, the changes were less marked, on the surface at least, than in the high schools although the drive for excellence, the enormous expansion of graduate education, a whole new range of community colleges, and a revived understanding of their social responsibility, when taken altogether, were scarcely less revolutionary. Indeed, American education finally achieved the position of being viewed from some quarters abroad as the model for a new age, a prestige it had never enjoyed before. The NCA and the other regional associations played an important part in most, if not all, of these developments.

Yet there would be little time for the enjoyment of past accomplishments. The problems of growth were nowhere near an end, particularly at the college level. An aspect of the unprecedented growth, one with which the Association had dealt hardly at all, was the great size American universities were reaching. This was itself the cause of an entire new range of criticisms about machine-like impersonality and bad teaching. The problem of optimum size, or how to adjust to bigness, had never really entered into accrediting procedures, although a possible sign of a trend was the NCA decision to consider university branches as separate institutions at a certain stage of their development.

Amid the pressures and frustrations which were the concomitants of size in the multiversities, new problems and issues were demanding immediate attention. These were urban poverty, racial discrimination, and the frustrations of the Viet Nam War, all of which, with countless local manifestations and complications, inevitably involved the high school, college, and university worlds. Should the NCA assume an activist role by setting out to become the originator and instrument of planned social change? Or should it limit itself to adjusting the schools and colleges it supervised to such changes as they occurred?

In the late 1960's the NCA appeared to be leaning toward the latter, partly because its resources in men and money were limited, and partly as a matter of principle. There was strong historical precedent in support of this position. It will be recalled that Horace Mann, a passionate abolitionist at heart, had kept his views to himself as long as he was officially associated with public education because he felt that to do otherwise would involve the schools in fruitless and damaging public controversy. Yet even prudence had its perils, for the strong feelings surrounding these new issues would make any choice or none at all a statement of position in the eyes of excited partisans. How could the Association take a stand for educational equality, for instance, without becoming the center of violent controversy in cities split into warring worlds of the shabby inner-city ghettoes and the gleaming suburbs?

Equally difficult and related problems were those surrounding the internal administration of educational institutions. Years of effort had freed most colleges and universities from improper interventions by boards of control or by self-interested pressure groups. Simultaneously the internal management had been broadened to include the faculty on decisions especially involving appointment, tenure, and curricula. Faculty power of this sort had been recognized for years and even encouraged by the Association, although the Board of Directors was still unwilling to acquiesce to the American Association of University Professors' most recent demand (1967) for an official role in accreditation, on the ground that this was "special interest" representation.[1] Even so, faculty representation in the NCA was not unrelated to the familiar patterns of evolving educational relationships and procedures.

An entirely new problem, however was that posed by the "militants," mainly students and young faculty, who demanded wholesale changes in the structure and management of education without regard to established standards. Their methods ranged from demonstrations to direct confrontation to get what they wanted, even to the extremity of destroying an institution. On many campuses the situation had reached an acute, near-crisis stage by the late 1960's. Some of the most prestigious universities in the land were brought to the verge of ruin—or so it seemed at the time— by a familiar pattern of "non-negotiable" demands, forcible occupation of buildings, clashes with police, and faction-torn faculties unable to decide on a course of action.

How long could an institution remain accredited if it were closed frequently or were even only half in operation because of disorders? How could an accrediting association approve courses developed and taught by students or other unqualifed persons after it had spent three quarters of a century improving faculty qualifications? Could it approve a curriculum literally forced on an institution by a militant minority who shouted down all dissent and otherwise insisted on their own conformities in violation of every tradition of academic freedom? Almost inevitably the NCA and other accrediting bodies would have such problems brought before them.

Problems of the high schools were no less intense although of a somewhat different order. On one level there was a sharpening

1. "The Professor and Accreditation," Panel Discussion, *AAUP Bulletin,* XLVII (Summer 1961), pp. 146-150; "The Role of the Faculty in the Accrediting of Colleges and Universities," *Ibid.,* LIII (Winter 1967), pp. 414-415; Joseph Semrow, "Faculty Participation in Policy Formation," *NCAQ,* XLII (Spring 1968), pp. 277-278.

conflict between a newly self-assertive teaching profession and the old ruling hierarchy of boards and administrators; teachers' unions were on the rise and even such traditionally non-militant bodies as the National Education Association were entering the fray. Salaries, conditions of employment, and curriculum were becoming subject to negotiation among all members of the working school community. High school students, undoubtedly stimulated by the example of their older counterparts in the universities, were also developing the symptoms of activism.

Another problem, still more or less on the horizon, although its outlines were apparent in New York and elsewhere, was associated with the demand for direct community management of individual schools without regard for the usual canons accepted by either faculty or administration. Justified in the name of educational "relevancy" and civil liberty, it threatened the freedom of teaching that the unions were on the verge of winning.

Although no specific emergency had yet arisen in 1969 requiring drastic action or specific statement of policy on most of such questions, the Association was in its deliberate way moving toward the necessary readjustments. As long ago as the middle 1950's it had given some indication of the course of action to be expected when it "permitted" the Little Rock High Schools to "resign" their memberships in the Association when they were closed in an effort to evade the legal obligation to desegregate. In more recent years various members of the Secondary Commission and its secretary participated in or sat as observers at various conferences to discuss the implications of such problems as *de facto* segregation in the cities or the consequences of direct community rule. To some degree at least Section III-D in *Policies and Criteria for Secondary Schools* offered an entering wedge and possibly a measure of NCA support for the forces out to "democratize" the schools. It states that

> The working relationship between the board of education and the administrative head of the system, between the administrative head of the system and the principal of the secondary school, and between principal and staff shall be such as to insure cooperative and effective administration.

> Administrative procedures shall be carried on by demo-
> cratic processes which utilize the abilities and contributions
> of staff members.

Increasing attention to the urban university and vocational institutes was likewise indicative of shifting emphases. Writing in
1964 on the subject, "Changing Concepts of Higher Education,"
Burns observed that the "urban university will share with the junior community college the honor and the challenge of carrying a
major portion of the load [of the democratization of higher
education.]"[2]

The extent of the Association's concern, as well as its direction,
was also evident in the increasing attention given to these problems in the *Quarterly* and at the annual meetings during 1968
and 1969. Within a brief period *Quarterly* titles included "A Fast
Express Named 'Militancy,'" "The Role of the Principal in Collective Negotiations," "Growing Tensions in Academic Administration," "Collective Bargaining for Teachers," "Faculty-Admin-
istrator Relationships," "Challenges to Institutional Integrity—
Internal Forces," "Challenges to Institutional Integrity—External
Forces," "Education and a Just Society," and "Toward a More
Relevant and Human Secondary Curriculum." Whitney Young,
executive secretary of the National Urban League, keynoted the
1969 annual convention and no fewer than eleven addresses or
panel discussions dealt with racial tensions, student violence, or
teacher-administrator relations.

It was none too soon. The fumbling and confusion so evident
in much of the academic community in the face of internal rebellion by a determined minority was an open invitation to some
form of intervention. If it did not come from the educational
community's own leaders acting together and backed by the prestige of accrediting power, it would almost certainly be imposed
by an irate public whose weapons were the purse and police.

In the 1970's a host of unfamiliar problems, products of social
change in the American community, confronted the educational

2. *NCAQ*, XXXVIII (Spring 1964), pp. 296-300. See also Norman Burns,
"Implications of By-Law Revisions," *NCAQ*, XLIV (Fall 1969), pp. 221-222.

establishment of the voluntary accrediting associations: good order in the university and fitting its students into a responsible and manageable role in the community, the developing financial crisis of the private colleges, the college and university obligation to the state and its involvement in the everyday world of affairs, the "relevance" of curricula, a rationale and method for educating "high-risk" students, and activism in the high schools. These were only some of the issues that promised to be of far larger import in the coming decades than the old-fashioned and now infrequent sort of failure that originated in arbitrary, uninformed boards, and dictatorial or unscrupulous administrators. The challenge to education was nothing less than "Renewing the Academic Community," the theme selected for the 1970 annual meeting of the North Central Association.

Bibliographical Note

The records of the North Central Association have been the basic source of information for this history. These include, first of all, the minutes and records of proceedings of the various bodies of the Association: the Board of Directors (various titles), the three Commissions, and the various executive committees of the Association and the Commissions. In addition, I have examined the reports of the annual meetings of the Association, including a considerable body of stenographic records that have been preserved, and the minutes of the annual meetings of the State Committees of the Commission on Secondary Schools.

All of the available publications and published records of the Association have also been examined, including files of the *North Central Association Quarterly*, NCA Today, files of mimeographed circulars and announcements, and reports of standing and *ad hoc* committees. Another essential part of the bibliography is the memories of a number of "old hands" in the Association who have been kind enough to read and comment on sections of the manuscript dealing with activities of which they had intimate knowledge (see acknowledgements in the preface).

In order to reduce the number of references, which would literally run into the hundreds, I have not cited any NCA records, except for articles and information taken from the *Quarterly*, which is readily available in any college library. Unless citation notes state otherwise, the information upon which this history is based is taken from NCA records, which are located in the central offices of the Association in Chicago.

The literature on accreditation has grown voluminously, especially since 1945. Professional and general educational periodicals have devoted much space to the subject. I have read or checked the articles on accreditation and related subjects that are listed in the usual bibliographical guides. It would be more pretentious than useful to name them all, since much of the material is repetitious; those that have proved useful have been cited as footnotes to the text of this history.

Various aspects of accreditation have also been given detailed treatment in doctoral dissertations. Among the more useful have been the following: Maynard D. Cochrane, "A Critical Analysis of Changes from 1950 through 1964 in the Policies and Criteria for Approval of Secondary Schools in the North Central Association of Colleges and Secondary Schools" (Ph.D. dissertation, University of Wyoming, 1964); Maurice D. Conroy, "A Study of Accreditation and Graduation Requirements of the Secondary Schools of the Northwest Association of Secondary and Higher Schools" (Ph.D. dissertation, University of Utah, 1950); Alphonsus Francis Diederich, "A History of Accreditation, Certification, and Teacher Training in Catholic Institutions of Higher Learning in California" (Ph.D. dissertation, University of California, Los Angeles, 1957); John F. Nevins, *A Study of the Organization and Operation of the Voluntary Accrediting Agencies* (Washington, D.C.: The Catholic University Press, 1959); Walter J. Ziemba, "Changes in the Policies and Procedures of the Accrediting Process of the Commission on Colleges and Universities of the North Central Association of Colleges and Secondary Schools, 1919-1958" (Ph.D. dissertation, University of Michigan, 1966).

An early general history of college-university accreditation which proved useful was the result of a series of studies on revision of standards sponsored jointly by the North Central Association and the General Education Board in the 1930's: *The Evolution of Higher Education,* Vol. I, *Principles of Accrediting Higher Institutions,* by George F. Zook and M. E. Haggerty (Chicago: University of Chicago Press, 1936). The most recent, and a more complete, general history is William K. Selden's *Accreditation: A Struggle Over Standards in Higher Education* (New York: Harper and Bros., 1960). It is somewhat less than a definitive study; there are fewer than a hundred pages of text; and accreditation of secondary schools is not included. The notes and bibliography are valuable references.

Another valuable compendium of general information, particularly on comparative practices among the regional associations and the states with respect to standards for teacher preparation, is the study of teacher accreditation and the history of the National Council for the Accreditation of Teacher Education (NCATE) prepared for the National Commission on Accrediting. *Accreditation in Teacher Education: Its Influence on Higher Education* by John Mayor and Associates was published by the Commission in 1965.

For the most part, however, the history of individual accrediting bodies is an almost neglected field. The histories that do exist have been written by people who were intimately concerned with their subject in an official capacity, with the usual virtues and shortcomings of that circumstance. The NCA pioneered the field when it published *A History of the North Central Association of Colleges and Secondary Schools, 1895-1945* (Ann Arbor, 1945) by Calvin O. Davis, for many years editor of the *NCA Quarterly*. This history was continued ten years later by Milo Bail, a former president of the Association, in an extended article entitled, "Six Decades of Progress."[1] Also in 1945 the history of the Southern Association was published in *The Southern Association Quarterly*.[2] A brief popular-style history of the college commission of the Middle States Association was published (mimeograph) in 1961.[3] To commemorate its 75th anniversary in 1960, the New England

1. *NCA Quarterly*, XXX (October 1955), pp. 169-207.
2. Guy E. Snavely, "A Short History of the Southern Association of Colleges and Secondary Schools," IX (November 1945), pp. 424-549. Snavely had been secretary-treasurer of the Southern Association from 1926 to 1936.
3. Ewald B. Nyquist, "Life Begins at Forty: A Brief History of the Commission," (November 1961, mimeographed, 52 pages). Nyquist had served as secretary and later chairman of the commission, 1948-1959.

Association published a short history (paper pamphlet) containing mainly a report of the activities of its annual meetings.[4] All of these sources have provided important information and suggested avenues of inquiry.

On a less specific level, general histories of education, histories of universities, and histories of voluntary non-accrediting associations[5] have provided the perspective that the institutional historian, like the biographer, may lose in his absorption in a relatively narrow subject. The fact that some highly regarded works in educational history[6] neglect the voluntary accrediting process almost entirely is itself a commentary that requires consideration by the historian. Finally, the popular periodicals and the daily press[7] have been invaluable guides to the public's response to specific issues and attitudes toward the accrediting associations.

4. Claude M. Fuess, *A Nutshell History of the New England Association of Colleges and Secondary Schools,* (Cambridge, 1960).

5. One of the best of such histories is Edgar Wesley, *NEA: The First Hundred Years; The Building of the Teaching Profession* (New York: Harpers, 1957).

6. See, for example, Frederick Rudolph, *The American College and University: A History* (New York: Alfred Knopf, 1962). In more than 500 pages, Rudolph mentions voluntary accreditation only once and the regional associations not at all.

7. See, for example, the New York *Times* on the Parsons "case" and the London *Times,* "American Accrediting Associations: Pillars of Independence," March 8, 1963.

APPENDIXES

By-Laws of the Association*

The purposes of the North Central Association of Colleges and Secondary Schools (hereinafter referred to as the "Association") shall be those stated in the Articles of Incorporation. The Association also shall have such powers as are now or may hereafter be granted by the General Not for Profit Corporation Act of the State of Illinois.

The Association shall have and continuously maintain in the State of Illinois a registered office and a registered agent, whose office is identical with such registered office, and may have other offices within or without the State of Illinois as the Board of Directors may from time to time determine.

The geographical territory of the Association shall consist of the states of Arizona, Arkansas, Colorado, Illinois, Indiana, Iowa, Kansas, Michigan, Minnesota, Missouri, Nebraska, New Mexico, North Dakota, Ohio, Oklahoma, South Dakota, West Virginia, Wisconsin, and Wyoming and/or such other areas as may be hereafter determined. Territory shall be excluded from or included within the jurisdiction of the Association only upon the recommendation of the Board of Directors and by the vote of the Association. The recommendation of the Board of Directors shall be based on substantial evidence indicating that the action recommended represents the desire of the *institutions* of the territory designated.

Section 1. *Classes.* The membership of the Association shall consist of three classes: (a) *member institutions;* (b) officers of the Association and members of the Commissions; and (c) honorary members. Only members of Class (a) are eligible to vote at official

---

* Subject to the approval of the Association at the business meeting to be held April 8, 1970. Proposed amendments appear in italics.

meetings of the Association, although members of Class (b) and (c) may vote if they are official representatives of an institution listed in (a).

Membership in the Association for *institutions* is voluntary and must be initiated by the legally designated governing body of the institution. Although all decisions of the Association bearing on the policy and management of *institutions* are advisory in character, the Association has the right to establish requirements for membership, to develop and establish criteria for the evaluation of *institutions,* and to establish and maintain all regulations and conditions for continued membership in the Association.

Section 2. *Admission and Termination of Membership.* Any *institution* which has been approved by the Association shall be admitted to membership on the payment of the annual dues. Such membership shall cease if at any time the *institution* withdraws or is removed from the approved list of the Association or if the annual dues are more than one year in arrears. Any lapse in membership shall date from July 1 next succeeding the Annual Meeting at which time action was taken or, if action removing the institution from the approved list of the Association is taken at some time other than the Annual Meeting, the lapse in membership shall date from the 90th day following the date of the action.

Section 3. *Officers and Commissions.* All individuals holding membership on commissions of the Association or serving as elected officers of the Association shall thereby become members of the Association.

Section 4. *Honorary Members and Privileges.* Honorary members shall be nominated by a committee on honorary members and elected by a two-thirds vote of the Board of Directors. Such individuals shall be honorary members of the Association and not honorary members of any particular commission.

Section 5. *Exemption from Dues.* Honorary members, officers of the Association, and members of the commissions shall not be required to pay dues as hereinafter defined.

ARTICLE V. MEETINGS OF THE ASSOCIATION

Section 1. *Attendance.* Members of the Association, honorary members, individuals officially connected with *an institution* which holds membership in the Association, and individuals who are officially connected with the state department of public instruction of a state which is included in the geographical territory of the Association, shall have the right to attend the meetings and to participate in the activities of the Association and of the various commissions. It shall be understood, however, that attendance at such meetings and participation therein shall be in accordance with the Articles of Incorporation, the By-Laws of the Association, and also with the policies adopted by the various commissions and by the Board of Directors.

Section 2. *Annual Meeting.* An annual meeting of the Association shall be held each year, beginning with the year 1963, commencing on such date and held at such time as the Board of Directors may prescribe and shall consist of as many sessions as the Board of Directors may prescribe.

Section 3. *Special Meetings.* Special meetings of the Association may be called by the president, by the Board of Directors, or by not less than ten percent of the members entitled to vote at such meeting.

Section 4. *Place of Meetings.* All meetings shall be held at a place to be designated by the Board of Directors. The Board of Directors may designate any place within the geographical territory of the Association as the place of meeting for any annual meeting or for any special meeting called by the Board of Directors. If no designation is made, or if a special meeting be otherwise called, the place of meeting shall be the registered office of the Association in the State of Illinois.

Section 5. *Notice of Meetings.* Written or printed notice stating the place, day and hour of any meeting of the Association shall be delivered either personally or by mail to each member not less than five or more than forty days before the date of such meeting by or at the direction of the President or the Secretary or persons calling the meeting. In case of a special meeting or one required by statute or by these By-Laws, the purpose for which the meeting is called shall be stated in the notice. If mailed, the notice of the meeting shall be deemed delivered when deposited in the United States mail addressed to the member at the address appearing on the records of the Association, with postage thereon prepaid.

Section 6. *Voting.* All votes at official meetings of the Association shall be member *institutions* only. Each member *institution* shall have only one vote on any question before the Association and this vote shall be cast by an officially designated representative.

Section 7. *Quorum.* Fifty voting members of the Association shall constitute a quorum for conducting business at any official meeting of the Association. If a quorum is not present at any such meeting, a majority of the members present may adjourn the meeting from time to time without further notice.

ARTICLE VI. BOARD OF DIRECTORS

Section 1. *General Powers.* The affairs of the Association shall be managed by its Board of Directors.

Section 2. *Number and Qualifications. There shall be 15 voting Directors who* need not be residents of the State of Illinois, but all elected Directors shall be officially and actively connected with *an institution* which holds membership in the Association or with a state department of education of a state in the geographical territory of the Association as defined in Article III.

Section 3. *Election and terms of Directors.* The Board of Directors shall consist of the President, the Vice-President, the President of the Association during the preceding year, the Secretary of the Association *ex officio* and without vote, the Treasurer *ex officio* and without vote, the Editor of Publications *ex officio* and without vote, and the chairman and secretary of each of the commissions established in Article VIII, provided that if the secretary of a commission is paid any compensation by the Association or a commission, he shall be an *ex officio* member of the Board of Directors and without vote. In addition to the chairman and secretary, each commission shall elect two members, and if the secretary is an *ex officio* member without vote, the commission shall also elect a third member. All terms of members elected by the commission shall be for a full four years. Each commission shall determine the method of election of its members of the Board of Directors.

Section 4. *Regular Meetings.* The annual meeting of the Board of Directors shall be held at the same place and immediately following the annual meeting of the Association. Such meetings shall be held without other notice than this By-Law.

The Board of Directors may provide by resolution the time and place, within the geographical territory of the Association, for the holding of additional regular meetings of the Board without other notice than such resolution.

Section 5. *Special Meetings.* Special meetings of the Board of Directors may be called by or at the request of the President or any four Directors. The person or persons authorized to call special meetings of the Board of Directors may fix any place, within the geographical territory of the Association, as the place for holding any special meeting of the Board called by them.

Section 6. *Notice of Special Meetings*. Notice of any special meeting by the Board of Directors shall be given at least five days previous thereto by written notice delivered personally or sent by mail or telegram to each Director at his address as shown by the records of the Association. If mailed, such notice shall be deemed to be delivered when deposited in the United States mail in a sealed envelope so addressed, with postage thereon prepaid. If notice be given by telegram, such notice shall be deemed to be delivered when the telegram is delivered to the telegraph company. Any Director may waive notice of any meeting. The attendance of a Director at any meeting shall constitute a waiver of notice of such meeting, except where the Director attends a meeting for the express purpose of objecting to the transaction of any business because the meeting is not lawfully called or convened. Neither the business to be transacted at, nor the purpose of, any regular or special meeting of the Board need be specified in the notice or waiver of notice of such meeting unless specifically required by law or by these By-Laws.

Section 7. *Quorum*. A majority of the voting members of the Board shall constitute a quorum for the transaction of business at any meeting of the Board. If less than a majority of the Directors are present at a meeting, a majority of the Directors present may adjourn the meeting from time to time without further notice.

Section 8. *Manner of Acting*. The act of a majority of the voting Directors present at a meeting at which a quorum is present shall be the act of the Board of Directors. Informal action may be taken by the Board on matters submitted to its members by mail, such action to become effective upon receipt by the Secretary of written approval thereof by a majority, or in the case of election of new members by two-thirds of the Board.

Section 9. *Vacancies*. Any vacancy occurring in the Board of Directors and any Directorship to be filled by reason of any increase in the number of Directors, shall be filled by the Board of Directors, except that if a vacancy occurs due to the death or resignation of a Director elected or appointed by a commission, such vacancy shall be filled by the appropriate commission. A Director elected or appointed, as the case may be, to fill a vacancy shall be elected or appointed for the unexpired term of his predecessor in office.

Section 10. *Compensation*. Directors as such shall not receive any salary for their services. Nothing herein contained shall be construed to preclude any Director from serving the Association in any other capacity and receiving compensation therefor.

Section 11. *Duties and Responsibilities.*

a. The Board of Directors shall publish and distribute to the membership the NORTH CENTRAL ASSOCIATION QUARTERLY, which shall be the official organ of the Association, and such other publications as it may from time to time determine.

b. The Board of Directors shall receive from the Commission on *Institutions of Higher Education* the list of *higher institutions* recommended for membership in the Association and from the Commission on Secondary Schools the list of secondary schools recommended for membership in the Association. It shall submit such lists to the Association for final approval and shall publish in the NORTH CENTRAL ASSOCIATION QUARTERLY, the lists of *institutions* approved by the Association. The Board of Directors shall act for the Association between meetings of the Association on recommended changes in the list of member *institutions.*

c. *1. Requests for reconsideration of decisions of the Association shall be filed with the Executive Secretary of the Association not sooner than 10 days and not more than 30 days following the meeting at which the decisions were made and shall represent official action of the governing bodies of the institutions concerned. The basis for such requests for reconsideration shall be alleged bias, injustice, departure from established procedures, or factual error of sufficient magnitude to warrant reconsideration of the decision. Such allegations shall be supported by evidence in writing, submitted by the institution making the request.*

2. The Executive Secretary of the Association shall transmit a request for reconsideration to the Executive Secretary of the Commission concerned who shall submit the request to the administrative committee of that Commission.

3. The administrative committee of the appropriate Commission, or a committee appointed by the Chairman of the Commission which shall report its findings to the administrative committee, shall consider the allegations of bias, injustice, departure from established procedure, or factual error of sufficient magnitude to warrant reconsideration of the decision, and shall study the evidence submitted in writing by the institution. The administrative committee shall then submit to the Board of Directors of the Association its report and recommendations together with the allegations and the evidence received from the institution. Thereupon, the Board of Directors of the Association having considered the allegations, the supporting evidence, and the recommendations of the administrative committee, shall take final action on the request for reconsideration.

d. The Board of Directors shall submit to the Association for its information, the names of those persons elected by the respective commissions for membership therein, and certified to the Board of Directors, in accordance with the provisions of these By-Laws.

e. The Board of Directors shall approve and/or prepare the programs for the Annual Meeting of the Association, and provide for the publication of reports and proceedings.

f. The Board of Directors shall coordinate and publicize the work of the various commissions so as to further most effectively the purposes of the Association. The Board of Directors shall approve or disapprove, in advance, the proposed program of activities of each commission that may involve commitments by the Association.

g. The Board of Directors shall have the authority to approve all expenditures of funds and to require each commission to submit to it a budget, which shall be a complete forecast embracing (1) the program of activities, (2) the estimated receipts together with their sources, and (3) the estimated expenditure necessary to carry out the work of the commission.

h. At each Annual Meeting of the Association, the Board of Directors shall submit to the Association a detailed report of income and expenditures and, at the close of the fiscal year, require an official audit of all Association accounts to be made by an auditor selected by the Treasurer and approved by the Board of Directors. The audited report shall be published in the NORTH CENTRAL ASSOCIATION QUARTERLY.

ARTICLE VII. OFFICERS

Section 1. *Qualifications.* The officers of the Association shall be a President, a Vice-President, a Secretary, a Treasurer, and such other officers as the Board of Directors shall deem desirable. Such officers shall have the authority and perform the duties set forth in these By-Laws and prescribed from time to time by the Board of Directors. Any two or more offices may be held by the same person, except the offices of President and Secretary.

All elected officers of the Association and of the commissions shall be officially and actively connected with an *institution* which holds membership in the Association or with the state department of education of a state in the geographical territory of the Association as defined in Article III.

Section 2. *Election and Term of Office.* The President and Vice-President shall be elected at the Annual Meeting of the Association by a majority vote of those present and voting, for a single term of one year, and each shall hold office until his successor shall have been duly elected and shall have qualified.

Section 3. *Appointive Officers.* The Secretary, the Treasurer, and the Editor of Publications shall be appointed by the Board of Directors for terms of three years and each shall hold office until his successor shall have been duly appointed and shall have qualified.

Section 4. *Removal.* Any officer or agent appointed by the Board of Directors may be removed by the Board of Directors whenever in its judgment the best interests of the Association would be served thereby. Any officer or agent elected by the Association may be removed by the membership at a meeting called for that purpose. Such removal shall be without prejudice to the contractual rights, if any, of the persons so removed.

Section 5. *Vacancies.* A vacancy in any elective office by reason of death, resignation, removal, disqualification, or otherwise, may be filled by the Board of Directors for the unexpired portion of the term.

Section 6. *President.* The President shall preside at all meetings of the Association and of the Board of Directors. He may sign, with the Secretary or any other proper officer of the Association authorized by the Board of Directors, any deeds, mortgages, bonds, contracts, or other instruments which the Board of Directors have authorized to be executed, except in cases where the signing and execution thereof shall be expressly delegated by the Board of Directors, or by these By-Laws, or by statute, to some other officer or agent of the Association. In general, he shall perform all duties incident to the office and such other duties as may be prescribed by the Board of Directors from time to time.

Section 7. *Vice-President.* In the absence of the President, or in the event of his inability or refusal to act, the Vice-President shall perform the duties of the President and, when so acting, shall have all the powers of and be subject to all the restrictions upon the President. The Vice-President shall perform such other duties as from time to time may be assigned to him by the President or by the Board of Directors.

Section 8. *Secretary.* The Secretary shall keep the minutes of the meetings of the Association and of the Board of Directors, in books provided for that purpose; see that all notices are duly given in accordance with the provisions of these By-Laws or as required by law; be custodian of the corporate records and of the seal of the Association, and see that the seal of the Association is affixed to all documents, the execution of which, on behalf of the Association under its seal, is duly authorized in accordance with the provisions of these By-Laws; keep a register of the post-office address of each member which shall be furnished to the Secretary by such member; and, in general, perform all duties incident to the office of Secretary, and such other duties as from time to time may be assigned to him by the President or by the Board of Directors. He shall send, or cause to be sent, copies of minutes of meetings of the members, the Board and the commissions, as the case may be to such members, Directors, or commission members.

Section 9. *Treasurer.* If required by the Board of Directors, the Treasurer shall give a bond for the faithful discharge of his duties in such sum and with such sureties or surety as the Board of Directors shall determine. The expense of such bond shall be assumed by the Association. He shall have charge and custody of and be responsible for all funds and securities of the Association, receive and give receipts for money due and payable to the Association from any source whatsoever, and deposit all such moneys in the name of the Association in such banks, trust companies, or other depositories as shall be selected in accordance with the provisions of Article XI of these By-Laws. In general, he shall perform all the duties incident to the office of Treasurer and such other duties as from time to time may be assigned to him by the Board of Directors.

ARTICLE VIII. COMMISSIONS

Section 1. *Classification of Commissions.* Class (a) membership of the Association, as provided for in Article IV, Section 1 of these By-Laws, shall be further divided into (1) member *institutions of higher education* and (2) member secondary schools. Each of these subdivision of Class (a) membership shall be governed by its respective commission as set forth in these By-Laws. Members of both of these subdivisions shall be included on the Commission on Research and Service.

The Board of Directors shall appoint the initial members of each commission who shall hold office until the first Annual Meeting of the Association. The number of members so appointed to each commission shall be determined by resolution of the Board of Directors. Thereafter, election to a commission shall be as provided in the Rules of Procedure adopted by each of the commissions, not inconsistent with these By-Laws.

Section 2. The Commission on *Institutions of Higher Education.* There shall be a Commission on *Institutions of Higher Education* which shall group the member institutions of higher education by geographic districts and type of institution, the number and boundaries of the districts and the basis for grouping the types of institutions to be determined by the Commission.

The Commission on *Institutions of Higher Education* shall consist of representatives of its member institutions elected by the Commission subject to the approval of the Association, and three representatives designated by the Commission on Secondary Schools from among the membership of that Commission. Election of the members of the Commission on *Institutions of Higher Education* shall be in accordance with a formula adopted by the Commission which shall provide for representation by district and by type of institution. Election shall be for a term of four years with one-fourth of the members being elected annually. For a period of one year members shall not be eligible for re-election, except that a member of the Executive Board of the Commission on *Institutions of Higher Education* shall continue on the Commission as an added member until the expiration of his term on the Board.

The Commission shall have a Chairman, a Secretary, and Executive Board, and such other boards, committees, and officers as it deems appropriate. It shall adopt such Rules of Procedure, not inconsistent with these By-Laws, as may be necessary to elect its members to the Board of Directors and to the Association, elect members and officers of the Commission, elect and/or appoint officers and members of the Executive Board, and to discharge all duties and responsibilities of the Commission.

The Commission on *Institutions of Higher Education* shall prepare policy statements, subject to the approval of the Board of Directors, for the guidance of member and non-member *institutions of higher education;* receive and consider applications from *institutions of higher education* for membership in the Association and, in connection therewith, to make surveys and conduct examinations; request periodic reports from member institutions and make surveys and conduct examinations of such members; prepare a list of *institutions of higher education* recommended to the Association for accrediting; certify to the Board of Directors the persons elected to membership on the Commission and the proposed budget of the Commission; make and publish studies of educational problems approved by the Board of Directors; assist *institutions of higher education* in the territory served to strengthen their respective programs; and perform such other services, activities, and duties as the Board of Directors may from time to time prescribe.

Section 3. *The Commission on Secondary Schools.* There shall be a Commission on Secondary Schools which shall have a Chairman, a Secretary, an Administrative Committee, and such other boards, committees, and officers as it deems appropriate. It shall adopt such Rules of Procedure, not inconsistent with these By-Laws, as may be necessary to elect its members to the Board of Directors of the Association, elect members and officers of the Commission, elect and/or appoint officers and members of the Administrative Committee, elect or appoint its three representatives to the Commission on *Institutions of Higher Education* and to discharge all duties and responsibilities of the Commission.

The Commission on Secondary Schools shall consist of the members of the State Committees of each of the states comprising the geo-graphic territory of the Association, the members of the American Dependents' Schools Committee, and the members of the Administrative Committee.

The Commission on Secondary Schools shall establish policies and criteria for membership of secondary schools subject to the approval of the Board of Directors, and assist those secondary schools seeking membership in the Association; receive and consider annual reports from member schools and applications for membership from secondary schools within the geographic territory of the Association and from American Dependents' Schools operated in territory outside of the United States; make all necessary examinations and evaluations of member schools or applicants; prepare a list of secondary schools recommended to the Association for accreditation; certify to the Board of Directors the persons elected to membership in the Commission and the proposed budget of the Commission; conduct workshops on current problems at both state and regional levels; establish committees to study matters of common concern to secondary schools; promote improved high school-college relations; interpret secondary education to students, teachers, colleges and universities, and the general public; stimulate, through the accrediting process, the improvement of secondary education; and perform such other services, activities, and duties as the Board of Directors may from time to time prescribe.

Section 4. *The Commission on Research and Service.* There shall be a Commission on Research and Service which shall have a Chairman, *a Vice-Chairman,* a Secretary, a Steering Committee, and such other boards, committees and officers as it deems appropriate. It shall adopt such Rules of Procedure, not inconsistent with these By-Laws, as may be necessary to elect its members to the Board of Directors of the Association; appoint or elect members and officers of the Steering Committee; and discharge all duties and responsibilities of the Commission.

The Commission on Research and Service shall consist of twenty-four members, *exclusive of the officers of the Steering Committee, and the immediate past Chairman,* equally divided between (a) persons selected from the *member institutions of higher education* and (b) persons selected from the *member* secondary schools *elected by the Commissions of which their institutions are affiliated,* subject to the approval of the Board of Directors. Each member of the Commission shall be *selected* for a term of three years, four members from each of the two groups represented being *selected* annually. No member of the Commission shall serve more than two consecutive three-year terms.

The Steering Committee of the Commission shall consist of the Chairman, Vice-Chairman, Secretary (each elected for a two-year term), immediate past Chairman and six members of the Commission, one representing each of the two groups represented in each class as determined by termination date of three-year term of office. To be eligible for an office on the Steering Committee, the candidate must have had experience as a Commission member. If a vacancy on the Commission occurs as the result of the election to an office, that vacancy shall be filled by the appropriate Commission for the balance of the unexpired term.

The Commission on Research and Service shall *itself* initiate, plan and carry forward studies in the fields of educational and institutional research and service pertaining to institutions of higher education and secondary schools, subject to the approval of the Board of Directors; engage in such research study or activity as either of the other Commissions may request, subject to the approval of the Board of Directors; report its findings to the appropriate Commission or Commissions and to the Association as directed by the Board of Directors; submit its proposed budget to the Board of Directors for approval; certify to the Board of Directors the persons elected to membership on the Commission *and to offices on the Steering Committee;* furnish leadership in interpreting its research findings and focusing attention on problems in need of study and consideration; and perform such other services, activities, and duties as the Board of Directors may from time to time prescribe.

The Steering Committee shall conduct the business affairs of the Commission between meetings of the full Commission; assume leadership in reviewing proposals for research and study to determine their relevance to the purposes and functions of the Association; screen all problems and issues referred from the other Commissions and/or from any other source; implement Ad Hoc Committees to explore and study acceptable educational problems and issues; involve each member of the Commission, insofar as possible, in the activities of the Commission through membership on the Steering Committee or participation on the various Ad Hoc Committees.

ARTICLE IX. COMMITTEES OF THE ASSOCIATION

Section 1. *Nominating Committee.* No less than one month prior to the Annual Meeting of the Association, the President shall appoint, subject to the approval of the Board of Directors, a committee of five persons, designating one as chairman, whose duty it shall be to nominate qualified persons for election to the offices of president and vice-president and to any office not elsewhere provided for in these By-Laws. The Committee shall report its nominations to the membership assembled at least twenty-four hours prior to the meeting at which the election of officers takes place. Persons not members of the Board of Directors may be appointed as members of the Nominating Committee.

Independent nominations may also be made upon the written petition of any ten member institutions of the Association, such list of persons so nominated to be filed with the Secretary not less than twelve hours prior to the beginning of the session at which the election of such officers is to take place.

Section 2. *Other Committees.* Other committees, not having or exercising the authority of the Board of Directors in the management of the Association, may be designated by resolution adopted by a majority of the Directors present at a meeting at which a quorum is present. Persons may be designated as committee members who are not members of the Board of Directors. Members of such committees shall be appointed by the President and one of the members designated as chairman.

ARTICLE X. BOOKS AND RECORDS

The Association shall keep correct and complete books and records of account and shall also keep minutes of the proceedings of the Association, of the Board of Directors, and of the various commissions. It shall keep at the registered or principal office of the Association a record giving the names and addresses of *those member institutions entitled to vote. All books and records of the Association may be inspected by any member, or his agent or attorney, for any proper purpose at any reasonable time.*

ARTICLE XI. CONTRACTS, CHECKS, FUNDS, AND GIFTS

Section 1. *Contracts.* The Board of Directors may authorize any officer or officers, agent or agents, of the Association to enter into any contract or execute and deliver any instrument in the name of and on behalf of the Association and such authority may be general or confined to specific activities, except that the Board of Directors may not incur indebtedness in excess of annual income of the Association from fees and dues for the immediately preceding fiscal year without the approval of the Association.

Section 2. *Checks, Drafts, Etc.* All checks, drafts, or other orders for the payment of money, notes, or other evidences of indebtedness, issued in the name of the Association shall be signed by such officer or officers, agent or agents, of the Association, and in such manner as shall from time to time be determined by resolution of the Board of Directors. In the absence of such a determination by the Board of Directors, such instrument shall be signed by the Treasurer and counter-signed by the President or Vice-President of the Association.

Section 3. *Deposit of Funds.* All funds of the Association shall be deposited from time to time to the credit of the Association in such banks, trust companies, or other depositories as the Board of Directors may select.

Section 4. *Gifts.* The Board of Directors may accept, on behalf of the Association, any contributions, gifts, grants, bequests, or devises for the general purposes or for any special purpose of the Association.

ARTICLE XII. DUES

The Board of Directors, subject to the approval of the Association, shall determine from time to time the amount of annual dues or fees which shall be paid by each member *institution*.

ARTICLE XIII. FISCAL YEAR

The fiscal year of the Association shall begin on the first of July of each year and end on the thirtieth day of June next succeeding.

ARTICLE XIV. SEAL

The Board of Directors shall provide a corporate seal which shall be in the form of a circle and shall have inscribed thereon the name of the Association and the words, "Corporate Seal, Illinois."

ARTICLE XV. WAIVER OF NOTICE

Whenever any notice whatever is required to be given under the provisions of the General Not for Profit Corporation Act of the State of Illinois, or under the provisions of the Articles of Incorporation or the By-Laws of the Association, a waiver thereof, in writing, signed by the person or persons entitled to such notice shall be deemed equivalent to the giving of such notice.

ARTICLE XVI. AUTHORITY

Robert's Rules of Order Revised shall govern all meetings of the Association, the Board of Directors, and the commissions insofar as they are applicable and not inconsistent with the statutes of the State of Illinois, the Articles of Incorporation, these By-Laws, and the Rules of Procedure adopted by the various commissions.

ARTICLE XVII. AMENDMENTS TO BY-LAWS

These By-Laws may be amended or repealed and new By-Laws may be adopted upon recommendation of three-fourths of the Directors present at any regular or at any special meeting, subject to the ratification by the Association, providing that at least thirty days' prior written notice is given the Association of intention to amend, repeal, or adopt new By-Laws at such meeting.

Presidents of the Association

* Presided at Annual Meeting
** Deceased

** 1922   L. D. COFFMAN, President of the University of Minnesota

** 1923   M. H. STUART, Principal of Technical High School, Indianapolis

** 1924   C. H. JUDD, Professor, University of Chicago

** 1925   E. L. MILLER, Assistant Superintendent of Schools, Detroit

** 1926   H. M. GAGE, President of Coe College

** 1927   J. D. ELLIFF, Professor, University of Missouri

** 1928   W. W. BOYD, President of Western College

** 1929   W. I. EARLY, Principal of the High School, Sioux Falls

** 1930   W. P. MORGAN, President of Western Illinois State Teachers College

** 1931   MERLE PRUNTY, Superintendent of Schools, Tulsa

** 1932   J. B. EDMONSON, Dean, School of Education, University of Michigan

** 1933   A. A. REED, University Examiner, University of Nebraska

1934   H. M. WRISTON, President of Lawrence College

** 1935   B. L. STRADLEY, University Examiner, The Ohio State University

** 1936   L. N. MCWHORTER, Assistant Superintendent of Schools, Minneapolis

** 1937   A. M. SCHWITALLA, Dean, School of Medicine, St. Louis University

** 1938   E. H. K. MCCOMB, Principal, Manual Training High School, Indianapolis

1939   A. W. CLEVENGER, High School Visitor, University of Illinois

** 1940   GEORGE A. WORKS, University Examiner, University of Chicago

** 1941   IRVING MAURER, President of Beloit College

** 1942   DEWITT MORGAN, Superintendent of Schools, Indianapolis

** 1943   CHARLES E. FRILEY, President of Iowa State College

** 1944   W. E. MCVEY, Superintendent of Public Schools, Harvey, Illinois

1945[1]   F. E. HENZLIK, Dean, Teachers College, University of Nebraska

** Deceased

1. A semi-centennial anniversary celebration was planned for the 1945 Annual Meeting. The meeting however was cancelled because war conditions made impossible the necessary transportation and hotel facilities. A skeletal meeting of the members of the Executive Committee and official representatives of each of the three Commissions took all necessary actions including a moratorium of

1946 F. E. HENZLIK, Dean, Teachers College, University of Nebraska

1947 R. NELSON SNIDER, Principal of South Side High School, Fort Wayne, Indiana

1948 JOHN R. EMENS, President of Ball State Teachers College, Muncie, Indiana

** 1949 JOHN E. FELLOWS, Dean of Admission and Registrar, University of Oklahoma

** 1950 CHARLES W. BOARDMAN, Professor of Education, University of Minnesota

1951 MATT L. ELLIS, President of Hendrix College, Conway, Arkansas

1952 GEORGE W. ROSENLOF, Director of Admissions, University of Nebraska

1953 MILO BAIL, President of University of Omaha, Nebraska

1954 EARL R. SIFERT, Supt. of Proviso Township High School, Maywood, Illinois

1955 EDGAR G. JOHNSTON, Professor of Education, Wayne University, Detroit

1956 J. EDGAR STONECIPHER, Director of Secondary Education, Des Moines Public Schools

1957 PAUL C. REINERT, S.J., President of St. Louis University

1958 LOWELL B. FISHER, Coordinator of University-School Articulation, University of Illinois

** 1959 T. H. BROAD, Director of Curriculum, Oklahoma City Public Schools

1960 WILLIAM R. ROSS, President of Colorado State College

1961 STEPHEN A. ROMINE, Dean, School of Education, University of Colorado

1962 J. FRED MURPHY, Principal, Broad Ripple High School, Indianapolis

1963 IRWIN J. LUBBERS, President of Hope College, Holland, Michigan

1964 RALPH C. JOHNSON, Principal, Wyandotte High School, Kansas City, Kansas

1965 CLYDE VROMAN, Director of Admissions, University of Michigan

1966 MARVIN C. KNUDSON, President of Southern Colorado State College

---

one year in the election of all Association officers and members of the three Commissions. (*North Central Association Quarterly,* Vol. XX, Number 1, July, 1945, pp. 1-6.)

** Deceased

1967 L. A. VAN DYKE, Professor of Education, University of Iowa

1968 HERBERT W. SCHOOLING, Dean of Faculties, University of Missouri

1969 EDWARD J. DRUMMOND, S.J., Vice President for Medical Center, St. Louis University

1970 ROBERT A. CROWELL, Associate Dean, College of Education, University of Arizona

Association Secretaries

1895-1898 F. L. Bliss, Principal, Detroit, Michigan
1898-1900 C. A. Waldo, Professor, Purdue University
1900-1902 F. N. Scott, Professor, University of Michigan
1902-1906 J. V. Denney, Professor, Ohio State University
1906-1915 T. A. Clark, Dean, University of Illinois
1915-1919 H. E. Brown, Principal, Kenilworth, Illinois
1919-1925 H. M. Gage, Professor, Coe College, Cedar Rapids, Iowa
1925-1931 J. B. Edmondson, Dean, University of Michigan
1931-1938 A. W. Clevenger, High School Visitor, University of Illinois
1938-1939 W. W. Haggard, Superintendent, Joliet, Illinois
1939-1951 G. W. Rosenlof, Professor, University of Nebraska
1951-1959 Charles W. Boardman, Professor, University of Minnesota
1959-1960 Robert J. Keller, Professor, University of Minnesota
1960— Norman Burns, Professor, University of Chicago

Association Treasurers

1895-1901 G. N. Carman, Director, Lewis Institute, Chicago
1901-1914 J. E. Armstrong, Principal, Chicago, Illinois
1914-1922 M. H. Stuart, Principal, Indianapolis, Indiana
1922-1928 W. I. Early, Principal, Sioux Falls, South Dakota
1928-1937 E. H. K. McComb, Principal, Indianapolis, Indiana
1937-1946 W. F. Shirley, Supt. of Schools, Marshalltown, Iowa
1946-1951 William E. McVey, Supt. of Schools, Harvey, Illinois
1951-1962 R. Nelson Snider, Principal, Fort Wayne, Indiana
1962— J. Fred Murphy, Principal, Indianapolis, Indiana

Association Honorary Members*

Position At Time Honored

W. BOYD ALEXANDER, Vice President, Antioch College

IRA L. BALDWIN, Special Assistant to the President, Univ. of Wisconsin

F. G. BLAIR, Illinois State Supt. of Public Instruction

HAROLD J. BOWERS, Deputy Supt., Ohio State Department of Education

OTIS W. CALDWELL, Director, Institute School Experimentation, Columbia University

GEORGE CARROTHERS, Director of the Bureau of Cooperation With Educational Institutions, University of Michigan

N. P. COLWELL, Secretary, Council on Medical Education, American Medical Association, Chicago

RUSSELL COOPER, Asst. Dean, College of Science, Literature, and the Arts, University of Minnesota

WALTER L. COOPER, Supt., J. Sterling Morton High School and Junior College, Cicero, Illinois

WILLIAM JOHN COOPER, United States Commissioner of Education

E. H. CRISWELL, Dean, College of Liberal Arts, University of Tulsa, Oklahoma

OTIS CROSBY, Asst. Director of Information, Detroit Public Schools

CALVIN O. DAVIS, Professor, University of Michigan

HARVEY H. DAVIS, Provost, University of Iowa

JOHN W. DAVIS, President, West Virginia State College at Institute

DAN H. EIKENBERRY, Professor, Ohio State University

ELMER ELLIS, President, University of Missouri

DONALD G. EMERY, Supt. of Schools, Shaker Heights, Ohio

H. W. FRANKENFELD, Registrar, University of South Dakota

CARL G. F. FRANZEN, Professor of Secondary Education, Indiana University

OLIVER K. GARRETSON, Professor of Secondary Education, University of Arizona

ALVA J. GIBSON, Supervisor of Administration, West Virginia State Department of Education

W. A. GREESON, Supt. of Schools, Grand Rapids, Michigan

PERRY GRESHAM, President, Bethany College, Bethany, West Virginia

JOHN C. HANNA, Supervisor of High Schools, Illinois State Department of Public Instruction

HENRY G. HARMON, President, Drake University

PAUL W. HARNLY, Asst. Supt. of Schools, Wichita, Kansas

* Honorary membership in the Association has been conferred on all past presidents, secretaries, and treasurers. This list cites additional Honorary Members who have made major contributions to education in general and to the advancement of the aims of the North Central Association.

182

CLARENCE B. HILBERRY, President, Wayne University, Detroit
GEORGE HILL, Professor of Education, Ohio University, Athens
J. A. HOLLEY, Dean, College of Education, Oklahoma State University, Stillwater
HORACE A. HOLLISTER, High School Visitor, University of Illinois
RAYMOND M. HUGHES, President, Iowa State College
REES H. HUGHES, President, Kansas State Teachers College, Pittsburg
W. H. JOHNSON, University of Kansas
THOMAS L. JONES, High School Visitor, University of Wisconsin
F. J. KELLY, Chief of the Division of Colleges and Professional Schools, U. S. Office of Education
LOUIS R. KILZER, Professor of Secondary Education, University of Wyoming
JOHN R. KIRK, President Emeritus, State Teachers College, Kirksville, Missouri
HARLAN C. KOCH, Asst. Dean, School of Graduate Studies, University of Michigan
RUSSELL F. LEWIS, First Asst. Supt., Wisconsin State Department of Public Instruction
JOHN E. MCADAM, Professor of Education, University of Iowa
REV. DANIEL J. MCHUGH, De Paul University of Chicago
JULIAN L. MALINE, S.J., Professor of Education, West Baden College of Loyola University, West Baden Springs, Indiana
C. L. MEES, President, Rose Polytechnic Institute, Terre Haute, Indiana
HAROLD METCALF, Supt., Bloom Township High School and Community College, Chicago Heights, Illinois
SISTER MARY A. MOLLOY, President, College of St. Teresa, Winona, Minnesota
FRANK MOSSMAN, President, Morningside College, Sioux City, Iowa
M. G. NEALE, Professor of Education, University of Minnesota
JOHN E. NELSON, Dean of Graduate School, University of Kansas
JESSE H. NEWLON, Director, Lincoln Experimental School, Teachers College, Columbia University
MORGAN RICHARD OWENS, Arkansas State Department of Education, Little Rock
C. I. PONTIUS, Chancellor, University of Tulsa, Oklahoma
SAMUEL QUIGLEY, University of Texas, Houston
FLOYD W. REEVES, Professor of Educational Administration, Michigan State University
FRANCIS ROSENCRANCE, Dean, College of Education, Wayne State University, Detroit
JOHN DALE RUSSELL, Director, Bureau of Institutional Research, New York University
JOHN RUFI, Professor of Education, University of Missouri
MOTHER MARY SAMUEL, Principal, St. Clara Academy, Sinsinawa, Wisconsin

John L. Seaton, President, Albion College, Albion, Michigan

Raymond Shoop, Missouri State Department of Vocational Education, Jefferson City

Floyd L. Simmons, Principal, East High School, Cleveland, Ohio

Jake Smart, Assistant Superintendent in Charge of Instruction, State Department of Public Instruction, Oklahoma City, Oklahoma

Blair Stewart, President, Associated Colleges of the Midwest, Chicago

Bland L. Stradley, University Examiner, Ohio State University

Ralph Stinson, Director of Accreditation and Field Services, Kansas State Department of Education

Miss Marian Talbot, Dean Emerita, University of Chicago

W. O. Thompson, President Emeritus, Ohio State University

Louis W. Webb, Professor of Education, Northwestern University

Elmer M. Weltzin, Director of Graded Elementary and Secondary Schools, Minnesota State Department of Education

Allen S. Whitney, Dean of School of Education, University of Michigan

A. L. Whittenberg, Secretary, State Examining Board, Department of Public Instruction, Springfield, Illinois

First Published List of Accredited Secondary Schools*

Colorado: Colorado Springs, Cripple Creek, Greeley, Kenyon City, La Junta, Leadville, Pueblo (No. 1, No. 20), Trinidad. (9 schools)

Illinois: Aurora (East), Aurora (West), Bloomington, Chicago (Austin, Calumet, Englewood, Hyde Park, Jefferson, John Marshall, Joseph Medill, Lake, Lake View, North West Division, Robert Waller, South Chicago, South Division, William McKinley) Clyde, De Kalb, Dixon (South), Elgin, Evanston, Harvey, Joliet, La Grange, Moline, Oak Park, Ottawa, Peoria, Pontiac, Princeton, Rockford, Rock Island, Sterling. (34 schools)

Indiana: Fort Wayne, Frankfort, Howe Military School, Indianapolis (Shortridge, Manual Training), Michigan City, Rensselaer. (7 schools)

Iowa: Boone, Cedar Rapids, Council Bluffs, Davenport, Des Moines (West), Fort Dodge, Grinnell, Le Mars, Marshalltown, Ottumwa, Sioux City. (11 schools)

Michigan: Ann Arbor, Adrian, Alpena, Bay City, Battle Creek, Calumet, Coldwater, Detroit (Central, Eastern, University School, Home and Day School), Grand Haven, Grand Rapids, Hancock, Iron Mountain, Kalamazoo, Lansing, Menominee, Marquette, Muskegon, Mt. Clemens, Monroe, Marshall, Saginaw (West Side, East Side), St. Joseph, Traverse City, Ypsilanti. (28 schools)

Minnesota: Duluth, Minneapolis (Central, East Side), St. Paul (Central, Cleveland, Humboldt). (6 schools)

Missouri: Columbia (Bliss Military Academy), Kansas City (Central, Manual Training, Westport), Kirkwood, St. Louis (Central, William McKinley, Washington University Training School). 8 schools)

Nebraska: Beatrice, Kearney (Lincoln Academy), Omaha. (3 schools)

Ohio: Akron, Ashtabula, Bellefontaine, Cleveland (Central, East), Coshocton, Dayton, Delaware, East Cleveland, East Liverpool, Elyria, Findlay, Glenville, Greenville, Marion, Mansfield, Mt. Vernon, Piqua, Sandusky, Newark, Toledo, Troy, Van Wert, Xenia, Youngstown, Zanesville. (26 schools)

* From the *Proceedings* of the Association, 1904, pp. 48-49.

Wisconsin: Ashland, Chippewa, Eau Claire, Fort Atkinson, Janes-ville, Kenosha, La Crosse, Marinette, Marshfield, Merrill, Milwaukee (East, West, South, Downer Seminary), Oshkosh, Racine, Ryan, Sheboygan, Sparta, Stevens Point, Superior (Blaine, Nelson Dewey), Waukesha, Whitewater. (24 schools)

First Criteria for Accrediting Secondary Schools*

1. That the minimum scholastic attainment of all high school teach-ers be the equivalent of graduation from a college belonging to the North Central Association of Colleges and Secondary Schools, in-cluding special training in the subjects they teach, although such re-quirements shall not be construed as retroactive. . . .

2. That the number of daily periods of classroom instruction given by any one teacher should not exceed five, each to extend over a period of forty-five minutes.

3. That the laboratory and library facilities be adequate to the needs of instruction in the subjects taught as outlined in the report of the Commission.

4. That while the foregoing are exceedingly important factors affect-ing the quality of the work, the *esprit de corps*, the efficiency of the instruction, the acquired habits of thought and study, and the general intellectual and ethical tone of the school are of paramount impor-tance, and therefore only schools which rank well in these particulars, as evidenced by rigid, thorough-going, sympathetic inspection, should be considered eligible to the list.

* Appendix to the Proceedings of the Association, 1902, p. 36.

First Published List of Accredited Colleges and Universities*

Colorado: University of Colorado

Illinois: Augustana College; Bradley Polytechnic Institute, Junior College; Illinois College; Illinois Woman's College; Knox College; Lake Forest College; Lewis Institute, Junior College; Monmouth College; Northwestern University; Rockford College for Women; University of Chicago; University of Illinois; Wheaton College

Indiana: Indiana University; Purdue University; University of Notre Dame; Wabash College

Iowa: Coe College; Cornell College; Drake University; Grinnell College; Morningside College; Parsons College; Penn College; Simpson College; State University of Iowa; Upper Iowa University

Kansas: Baker University; College of Emporia; University of Kansas; Washburn College

Michigan: Olivet College, University of Michigan

Minnesota: Carleton College, Macalester College, University of Minnesota

Missouri: Central College; Park College; University of Missouri; Washington University; Westminster College

Nebraska: Doane College; University of Nebraska

North Dakota: Fargo College; University of North Dakota

Ohio: Case School of Applied Science; Denison University; German Wallace College; Heidelberg University; Kenyon College; Lake Erie College; Marietta College; Miami University; Mount Union-Scio College; Oberlin College; Ohio State University; Ohio University; Ohio Wesleyan University; Otterbein University; University of Cincinnati; Western College for Women; Western Reserve University

Oklahoma: University of Oklahoma

South Dakota: Dakota Wesleyan University; State University of South Dakota

Wisconsin: Beloit College; Carroll College; Lawrence College; Milwaukee-Downer College; Ripon College; University of Wisconsin

Unclassified List of Teachers' Colleges and Normal Schools Adopted for the Year 1913-1914: Illinois State Normal University; Southern Illinois Normal School; Western Illinois Normal School; Winona Normal School; Iowa State Teachers' College

* From the *Proceedings of the Association,* 1913, pp. 63-65.

First Criteria for Accrediting Colleges and Universities*

1. The minimum scholastic requirement of all college teachers shall be equivalent to graduation from a college belonging to this Association, and graduate work equal at least to that required for the master's degree. (A further statement *recommended* study beyond the M.A. degree.)

2. The college shall require for admission not less than fourteen secondary units, as defined by this Association.

3. The college shall require not less than 120 semester hours for graduation.

4. The college shall be provided with library and laboratory equipment sufficient to develop fully and illustrate each course announced.

5. The college, if a corporate institution, shall possess a productive endowment of not less than $200,000.

6. The college, if a tax-supported institution, shall receive an annual income of not less than $100,000.

7. The college shall maintain at least eight distinct departments in liberal arts, each with at least one professor giving full time to college work in that department.

8. The location and construction of the buildings, the lighting, heating and ventilation of rooms, the nature of the laboratories, corridors, closets, water supply, school furniture, apparatus, and methods of cleaning shall be such as to insure hygienic conditions for both students and teachers.

9. The number of hours of work by each teacher will vary in different departments. To determine this, the amount of preparation required for the class and the time needed for study to keep abreast of the subject, together with the number of students, must be taken into account; but in no case shall more than eighteen hours per week be required, fifteen being recommended as a maximum.

10. The college must be able to prepare its graduates to enter recognized graduate schools as candidates for advanced degrees.

11. The college should limit the number of students in a recitation or laboratory class to thirty.

12. The character of the curriculum, the efficiency of instruction, the scientific spirit, the standard for regular degrees, the conservatism in granting honorary degrees, and the tone of the institution shall also be factors in determining eligibility.

* *Proceedings* of the Association, 1912, p. 23.

NCA Accredited Institutions

Year and Class of Membership		Number of Accredited Institutions
1905	Secondary School	223*
1910	Secondary School	698
1915	College and University	125**
	Secondary School	1047
1920	College and University	188
	Secondary School	1353
1925	College and University	238
	Secondary School	1797
1930	College and University	279
	Secondary School	2336
1935	College and University	282
	Secondary School	2580
1940	College and University	295
	Secondary School	2906
1945	College and University	312
	Secondary School	3033
1950	College and University	356
	Secondary School	3130
1955	College and University	380
	Secondary School	3343
1960	College and University	432
	Secondary School	3580
1965	College and University	485
	Secondary School	3730
1969	College and University	554
	Secondary School	3819

* The first list of accredited secondary schools was published in 1904.
** The first list of accredited colleges and universities was published in 1913.

RECEIPTS AND EXPENDITURES AT
FIVE-YEAR INTERVALS

YEAR	RECEIPTS INCLUDING BALANCE FROM PRECEDING YEAR	EXPENDITURES	BALANCE AT YEAR'S END
1898**	$ 361	$ 348	$ 13
1900	492	348	144
1905	467	349	118
1910	901	615	286
1915	1,256	975	281
1920	6,925	4,372	2,553
1925	19,481	10,719	8,762
1930	37,582	17,805	19,777
1935	62,088	23,699	38,389
1940	75,623	38,916	36,707
1945	51,037	39,083	11,954
1950	110,666	73,658	37,008
1955	196,357	138,052	58,305
1960	211,639	156,338	55,301
1965	301,652	250,916	50,736
1969	512,586	403,586	109,000

* These figures represent administration funds and do not include grants from other sources for special projects.

** The first year that a treasurer's report was published.

Index

Deutsch, Harold, *America's Stake in Western Europe* (later revised and retitled *The New Europe, The Common Market, and the United States*), 20

Draper, A. S., x

Evaluative Criteria. See Accreditation, secondary schools

Evaluation Guide for Junior High Schools. See Accreditation, secondary schools

Evaluation Guide for Secondary Schools, 109

Federal aid to education, 8-9, 63-66, 85, 88, 127
  Agency for International Development (AID), 65
  Atomic Energy Commission, 65
  Department of Defense, 65
  Economic Opportunity Act (1964), 65
  Elementary and Secondary Education Act (1965), 58
  Higher Education Facilities Act (1963), 66, 85
  Manpower Development and Training Act (1962), 65
  National Aeronautics and Space Administration, 65
  National Defense Education Act (1958), 58, 64
  National Institutes of Health, 65
  National Science Foundation, 65, 88
  Office of Vocational Rehabilitation, 65
  Peace Corps, 65
  Public Health Service, 65

Veterans' Readjustment Act (1944) (GI Bill), 8

Vocational Education Act (1963), 65

Federation of Regional Accrediting Commissions of Higher Education (FRACHE), 70-72, 93, 113

Fiftieth Anniversary of the Association, 1-10

Finances of the Association
  Association income and expenditures, 59
  funds for projects, 128
  membership dues for colleges and universities, 94
  membership dues for secondary schools, 59, 109
  receipts and expenditures at five-year intervals, 190

Forbes, F. A., x

Ford Foundation, 20-21, 44, 56

Foreign Affairs Subcommittee, 20. *See also* Foreign Relations Project

Foreign Policy Association, 126

Foreign Relations Project, 121, 125-127

Geiger, Louis G., xix

General Educational Development Tests, 44

Gibson, Alva, 68

Goodlad, John, 103

Great Society, the, 104

Guidance and counseling in high schools, 18. *See also* Commission on Research and Service and Accreditation, secondary schools

Hamtramck (Michigan) High School, 51-52